50 FEARLESS WOMEN

WHO MADE AMERICAN HISTORY

D0061582

50 FEARLESS WOMEN

WHO MADE AMERICAN HISTORY

AN AMERICAN HISTORY BOOK FOR KIDS

JENIFER BAZZIT

ILLUSTRATED BY STEFFI WALTHALL

ROCKRIDGE
PRESS

For general information on our other products and services or to obtain technical support, please contact our Customer Care Department within the United States at (866) 744-2665, or outside the United States at (510) 253-0500.

Rockridge Press publishes its books in a variety of electronic and print formats. Some content that appears in print may not be available in electronic books, and vice versa.

Interior and Cover Designer: Stephanie Sumulong
Art Producer: Michael Hardgrove
Editor: Laura Bryn Sisson
Production Manager: Holly Haydash
Production Editor: Melissa Edeburn

Illustrations © Steffi Walthall, 2019

Author photo courtesy of Joshua Pound
Illustrator photo courtesy of Clarence Goss

ISBN: Print 978-1-64611-103-9 | eBook 978-1-64611-104-6

R0

This book is dedicated to my
precious grandma, Allne Pound.
She desperately wanted to complete her education
by attending high school. However, her life as the
daughter of a sharecropper in rural Oklahoma during
the Great Depression made that dream impossible.

CONTENTS

INTRODUCTION VIII

BIOGRAPHIES:

INTRODUCTION

The pages of social studies textbooks are filled with the stories of men who shaped the history of the United States with their political decisions, brave deeds, and admirable actions, but those stories are only part of that history. Countless American women labored and sacrificed to establish this country and improve the treatment of its citizens, and they proved themselves to be more than merely wives, mothers, daughters, and sisters.

It is humbling to think of the millions of women whose names and contributions are lost to history. Without them, however, we would not have this great nation to call home. The 50 women I chose to highlight in this book come from all walks of life, races, cultural backgrounds, and fields of study, and they represent different time periods in American history. Whether you are familiar or unfamiliar with the women in this book, you will certainly find relatable qualities and inspiration in reading their stories.

The captivating women featured in this book span centuries, from the earliest colonial settlements to women of the 21st century. You will learn about Anne Hutchinson, a woman who refused to keep quiet about her beliefs despite the consequences. Later, you will be inspired by Harriet Tubman, who not only escaped slavery but also risked her life time and again to help others journey to freedom. The story of Sally Ride, the first American woman in space, will encourage you to explore new frontiers.

Organized chronologically by the period of their achievements, each incredible woman's story will also show you American history as it unfolded. A timeline will help you follow historical events that occurred during each woman's lifetime. A sidebar will help you understand the historical context for each woman's story. Find the meaning of words set in **bold** in the glossary (see pages 151 to 153).

Although you may not agree with the opinions or actions of a particular woman, you'll find it worthwhile to further investigate her life to find out why she made the choices she did. Learning about opposing viewpoints leads to a more open, educated mind.

It is vital that we include the accomplishments and contributions of women in the study of United States history. We can learn a great deal by exploring the actions of the women who shaped that history and by examining the history that shaped them.

POCAHONTAS
(CA. 1597-1617)

POWHATAN WOMAN LINKED TO AMERICA'S COLONIAL HERITAGE

Pocahontas, the clever and brave daughter of a powerful chief, was instrumental in creating peace between her people and early English settlers.

Powhatan, paramount chief of the Powhatan tribes inhabiting the Chesapeake Bay region, welcomed a daughter, Matoaka, around 1597. Although she was one of many children, she was favored by her father, earning the nickname Pocahontas, which means "playful one."

The earliest written mention of Pocahontas is in an account of a 1607 incident by English Captain John Smith, a leader of the Jamestown settlement. The captain reported that a warrior stood over him, ready to smash his skull. Pocahontas placed her head upon the captain's head, seemingly stopping the execution. Historians have later questioned the accuracy of Captain Smith's report and whether the incident was actually a ritual or even completely fabricated. Whether Captain Smith misunderstood what happened or made up the story, we will never know.

During Jamestown's early years, Pocahontas visited the settlement often, bringing food items and delivering messages from her father. Pocahontas stopped visiting Jamestown when settlers violently demanded more food from the Powhatan people, and for the next few years, there is no mention of her in English records. Then in 1613, Pocahontas was kidnapped and held for ransom. Chief Powhatan met many of the settlers' demands.

Her time in captivity was likely traumatic. While held hostage, she met John Rolfe, who told Jamestown's governor that he wished to marry her. Pocahontas sent word

1585—THE ROANOKE COLONY, THE FIRST ENGLISH SETTLEMENT IN THE NEW WORLD, IS FOUNDED IN WHAT IS NOW NORTH CAROLINA.

1590—THE ROANOKE COLONY IS DISCOVERED MYSTERIOUSLY DESERTED.

to her father, and the years after this marriage were known as the "Peace of Pocahontas," a time of relative peace between the Jamestown settlers and the Powhatan tribes.

Along with her husband and young son, Pocahontas visited England as an **ambassador**. As the family was preparing for the return trip to Virginia, Pocahontas was stricken with a grave illness and died at the age of 20 or 21.

THE YEAR 1607 was a year of tremendous change in the Chesapeake Bay region of present-day Virginia. Some 100 English men and boys arrived and established a settlement they named Jamestown, for the then-king of England. Though inhabitants struggled with loss, starvation, and constant fear, Jamestown became the first permanent English settlement in what they called the New World.

COMING UP: ALMOST 20 YEARS AFTER POCAHONTAS BRAVELY FACED GREAT CHANGE, ANNE HUTCHINSON BRAVELY SPOKE HER MIND REGARDING RELIGIOUS CHALLENGES.

1620—PILGRIMS SETTLE IN PLYMOUTH.

1621—ACCORDING TO ACCOUNTS FROM THE TIME, THE FIRST THANKSGIVING CELEBRATION IS HELD IN PLYMOUTH.

ANNE HUTCHINSON
(1591-1643)
RELIGIOUS REFORMER

Women living in Anne Hutchinson's time were expected to remain quiet and **submissive**. Few women dared to challenge the authority of men, but Anne did just that. She is remembered today as an early American **feminist**.

Anne was born in England in 1591. Although she never attended school, her father ensured that she was well-versed in scripture.

As a young woman, Anne married William Hutchinson, a merchant from a respected family. Anne, along with her husband and many children, migrated to the Massachusetts

Bay Colony in 1634. Anne longed for the religious freedom that she thought would be readily available in the Puritan settlement across the ocean.

Anne was a trained midwife and used her knowledge to build relationships with the women in her new colony. Before long, she began to invite women to her home to discuss the sermons delivered

AFTER YEARS of persecution, Puritans sought religious freedom in the New World. On arrival in the Massachusetts Bay Colony, Governor John Winthrop set high expectations for the young settlement. His plan was to make Massachusetts Bay a "City upon a Hill," or a model town that would provide a good example for all.

by the beloved minister, John Cotton. The meetings grew to include both women and men when word spread about Anne's stirring interpretations of scripture.

Anne disagreed with many Puritan beliefs, and she did not hesitate to share her views. The colony's leaders were determined to put a stop to Anne's unauthorized meetings.

1625—NEW AMSTERDAM, LATER RENAMED NEW YORK, IS FOUNDED.

1630—JOHN WINTHROP LEADS A LARGE GROUP OF PURITANS TO SETTLE IN MASSACHUSETTS BAY.

While on trial for sharing beliefs that contradicted Puritan teachings, Anne refused to **recant** her statements and stop her religious meetings. She was found guilty, and her punishment was banishment from Massachusetts Bay.

The Hutchinson family sought refuge in the more tolerant colony of Rhode Island. Later, after the death of her husband, Anne and her family relocated to present-day New York, which was then under Dutch control. Soon after, the Dutch governor provoked a conflict with local Native American tribes, during which Hutchinson and most of her children were killed.

COMING UP: OVER A CENTURY AFTER ANNE HUTCHINSON USED HER VOICE TO SHARE HER BELIEFS, MERCY OTIS WARREN USED HER PEN TO FIGHT AGAINST THE UNFAIR POLICIES OF BRITISH LEADERS.

1636—PROVIDENCE, RHODE ISLAND, IS FOUNDED BY ROGER WILLIAMS AFTER HIS BANISHMENT FROM THE MASSACHUSETTS BAY COLONY.

1636—HARVARD COLLEGE IS FOUNDED.

MERCY OTIS WARREN

(1728-1814)

POLITICAL WRITER AND PROPAGANDIST OF THE AMERICAN REVOLUTION

During a time when women were expected to remain silent on political issues, Mercy Otis Warren wrote plays, poems, and other works to support the American colonists' struggle for independence from England.

Born into a wealthy Massachusetts family in 1728, Mercy Otis Warren lived in an era when girls typically received no formal education. However, due to her privileged circumstances, Mercy was able to attend lessons with her brothers and read a wide variety of books. Although 18th-century society discouraged the education of girls, Mercy's father encouraged her to continue learning, reading, and writing.

When Mercy married James Warren in 1754, he supported her writing efforts. James was active in politics and served in the Massachusetts legislature, which made it possible for Mercy to meet numerous patriot leaders. These relationships allowed her to increase her knowledge of the patriot movement.

While raising five sons, Mercy expressed her political opinions by writing multiple plays criticizing British leaders. These plays, published anonymously, appealed to a broad audience and helped raise support for the patriot cause.

WHILE THE NEW US Constitution was being debated, Mercy Otis Warren published a pamphlet encouraging changes to the document. She shared her opinion that the Constitution, as written, did not protect Americans from the government. Outspoken citizens, like Mercy, encouraged the addition of 10 amendments to the Constitution, known as the Bill of Rights, approved in 1791.

1752—BENJAMIN FRANKLIN'S KITE EXPERIMENT IS CONDUCTED.

1754—GEORGE WASHINGTON AND BRITISH TROOPS ATTACK FORT DUQUESNE AT THE BEGINNING OF THE FRENCH AND INDIAN WAR.

Mercy later published a collection of political poems and short plays under her own name. Additionally, Mercy became the first woman to author a history of the American Revolution, titled *History of the Rise, Progress and Termination of the American Revolution.*

Throughout her life, Mercy was outspoken in her belief that girls and women should be given educational opportunities. Mercy continued to write and correspond with friends and political acquaintances until her death at the age of 86.

COMING UP: A WRITER LIKE MERCY OTIS WARREN, AN ENSLAVED WOMAN NAMED PHILLIS WHEATLEY BECAME THE FIRST AFRICAN AMERICAN TO PUBLISH A BOOK OF POEMS.

1763—THE FRENCH AND INDIAN WAR ENDS.

1765—THE STAMP ACT CONGRESS IS HELD IN NEW YORK TO PROTEST TAXATION WITHOUT REPRESENTATION.

PHILLIS WHEATLEY
(CA. 1753-1784)

FIRST PUBLISHED AFRICAN AMERICAN POET, ENSLAVED WOMAN

Even more rare than a female writer in the 18th century was an enslaved female writer. Despite her status of **domestic** slave, Phillis Wheatley used her talent with words to undermine the view that people of African descent were **inferior**. She was the first African American in American history to publish a book of poems.

Born in The Gambia, Africa, Phillis was stolen from her homeland when she was about seven years old and transported to the American colonies to be sold. Once in

Boston, she was purchased by Susanna Wheatley, the wife of a successful tailor.

Phillis was treated relatively kindly by the Wheatley family, who shielded her from some of the more violent aspects of slavery. The family soon discovered that Phillis was intellectually gifted and began to invest a great deal of time and effort into her education. Susanna Wheatley's daughter, Mary, taught Phillis history, geography, classical literature, and more.

Phillis's first collection of poems, *Poems on Various Subjects, Religious and Moral,* was published in 1773.

In 1775, Phillis penned a letter to General George Washington containing a poem written in his honor. When Washington received the letter, he was pleased.

THE ABOLITIONIST movement began in the 18th century. People from all walks of life—black and white, rich and poor—tried to end slavery. **Abolitionist** efforts included speeches, written works, and group meetings. Phillis Wheatley's poems, along with the writings of others, fueled the abolitionist movement.

1770—BRITISH TROOPS FIRE INTO A CROWD OF COLONISTS DURING THE BOSTON MASSACRE.

1772—SAMUEL ADAMS ORGANIZES THE FIRST OF THE COMMITTEES OF CORRESPONDENCE IN BOSTON.

He wrote a letter of appreciation to Phillis and invited her to visit his headquarters in Massachusetts.

Phillis married a free black man, John Peters, in 1778. She continued to write poetry, but the small income she earned was not enough to save the couple from major financial hardship. With her husband in debtors' jail, Phillis died in poverty at the age of 31.

COMING UP: PHILLIS WHEATLEY INSPIRED THOUSANDS WITH HER BEAUTIFUL POEMS WHILE DEBORAH SAMPSON QUIETLY JOINED THE CONTINENTAL ARMY IN DISGUISE.

1773—THE SONS OF LIBERTY PROTEST THE TEA ACT BY TOSSING CRATES OF TEA INTO THE HARBOR DURING THE BOSTON TEA PARTY.

1774—THE FIRST CONTINENTAL CONGRESS MEETS.

DEBORAH SAMPSON
(1760–1827)

DISGUISED HERSELF AS A MAN TO SERVE IN THE AMERICAN REVOLUTION

During the American Revolutionary War, thousands of women trailed behind the Continental Army as camp followers, but they were not allowed to enlist as soldiers. A bold young woman, Deborah Sampson, joined the patriot army disguised as a man and served as a soldier for more than a year before her true identity was discovered.

In 1760, Deborah was born into a large family in Massachusetts. Upon the disappearance of her father at sea, Deborah's mother placed her with another family as an **indentured servant**. Deborah had a difficult start in life, but she educated herself by reading books. She completed her indenture contract and secured employment as a teacher at the age of 18.

A few years later, feeling restless in her small town, an adventurous young Deborah enlisted in the Continental Army under the name "Robert Shurtliff." Deborah served in multiple raids and expeditions.

Facing painful injuries, Deborah maintained her cover and was careful to never reveal her gender. On one occasion, she was shot in the leg but escaped from the hospital before a doctor could dress the wound. She removed the shrapnel from her leg on her own.

Deborah avoided anything that would cause her gender to be discovered. Unfortunately, she was stricken with a

MANY YOUNG MEN enlisted in the Continental Army hopeful that they would experience glory on the battlefield. Instead, soldiers endured small rations, a constant lack of supplies, and ever-present waves of disease sweeping through camp. During lulls in fighting, soldiers were kept busy digging trenches, cutting trees, drilling, and guarding the encampment.

1775—IN APRIL, PAUL REVERE RIDES AND THE BATTLES OF LEXINGTON AND CONCORD BEGIN THE REVOLUTIONARY WAR.

1775—IN JUNE, THE BATTLE OF BUNKER HILL IS FOUGHT IN BOSTON.

severe illness that left her unconscious. According to one account, her doctor discovered her gender but did not immediately reveal this information.

In October 1783, Deborah was granted an honorable discharge from the army after General John Paterson discovered her secret. Once home in Massachusetts, Deborah married and raised children on a small farm. In an attempt to support her struggling family, Deborah wrote a book about her experiences in the Continental Army and spoke to audiences in multiple cities. Deborah was granted a small military pension in 1819 and received it until her death in 1827.

COMING UP: DEBORAH SAMPSON SERVED HER COUNTRY UNDER AN ALIAS IN THE CONTINENTAL ARMY, WHILE ABIGAIL ADAMS USED HER POSITION AS FIRST LADY TO HIGHLIGHT INJUSTICE.

1776–*COMMON SENSE* BY THOMAS PAINE IS PUBLISHED, ENCOURAGING POPULAR SUPPORT FOR INDEPENDENCE.

1776–ON JULY 4, THE DECLARATION OF INDEPENDENCE IS APPROVED BY THE SECOND CONTINENTAL CONGRESS.

ABIGAIL ADAMS

(1744–1818)

WIFE OF SECOND PRESIDENT, JOHN ADAMS;
OUTSPOKEN PROPONENT OF EQUAL RIGHTS FOR ALL,
INCLUDING WOMEN AND ENSLAVED INDIVIDUALS

For most of American history, women were considered inferior to men and had few rights. Abigail Adams was ahead of her time in the belief that women should be provided educational opportunities and equal protection under the law. Additionally, she despised slavery and spoke out against the practice of holding individuals in bondage.

While Abigail never received a formal education, she learned a great deal through independent reading and study. She also helped her mother take care of sick and impoverished people in their community. This service gave Abigail a unique perspective on the struggles and needs of others.

In 1764, Abigail married John Adams, a young lawyer. As resistance to British policies grew, John became more involved in politics and traveled frequently. Through their frequent written correspondence, the couple discussed the issues of the day, and Abigail encouraged her husband to "remember the ladies" when participating in the First Continental Congress. She hoped that her husband and the men making decisions for the colonies would also protect the rights of women.

THE 18TH CENTURY was unkind to American women. They were denied educational opportunities, property rights, and voting rights. Unfortunately, Abigail Adams's plea to "remember the ladies" was ignored, and it took another 150 years before women were given the right to vote in the Nineteenth Amendment to the Constitution.

1781—BRITISH FORCES SURRENDER DURING THE LAST MAJOR BATTLE OF THE AMERICAN REVOLUTION.

1788—THE CONSTITUTION IS RATIFIED, OR APPROVED.

When her husband was elected president, theirs became the first family to live in the White House. Unlike the Washington family, John and Abigail Adams refused to use enslaved workers in the presidential residence.

Although Abigail passed away in 1818, her legacy of speaking out for equal rights continues to inspire Americans today.

COMING UP: WHILE THE OUTSPOKEN FIRST LADY ABIGAIL ADAMS WROTE INFLUENTIAL LETTERS TO HER HUSBAND AND OTHER POLITICAL LEADERS OF THE DAY, SACAGAWEA HELPED GUIDE THE CORPS OF DISCOVERY THROUGH THE NEWLY PURCHASED LOUISIANA TERRITORY.

1789—GEORGE WASHINGTON IS INAUGURATED IN NEW YORK CITY AS THE FIRST PRESIDENT OF THE UNITED STATES.

1791—THE FIRST BANK OF THE UNITED STATES IS CHARTERED.

SACAGAWEA
(CA. 1788-1812)

SHOSHONE (AND ONLY WOMAN) ON THE LEWIS AND CLARK EXPEDITION

Despite living in a time when the contributions of women often went unrecognized, Sacagawea, a knowledgeable Shoshone woman, became a famous figure in our nation's history.

Sacagawea was born into the Shoshone tribe around 1788. She grew up exploring her home in the Rocky Mountain region of present-day Idaho, where she learned a great deal about the plants and animals native to the area. As a young woman, Sacagawea was kidnapped by another tribe, the Hidatsa, and later forced to marry a French fur trader named Toussaint Charbonneau.

Sacagawea's path intersected with Meriwether Lewis and William Clark's expedition, known as the Corps of Discovery, at Fort Mandan, in present-day North Dakota. Lewis and Clark had been hired to explore and map the land recently acquired by the United States in the Louisiana Purchase.

DURING the post-Revolution years, the newly established United States was growing rapidly, and land was becoming scarce, causing all eyes to look west. In 1803, President Thomas Jefferson authorized the purchase of over 828,000 square miles of land controlled by France, known as the Louisiana Territory. The Louisiana Purchase instantly doubled the size of the United States.

Charbonneau was hired as a translator for the expedition and began the voyage accompanied by Sacagawea, then only about 16 years old. Both Charbonneau and Sacagawea spoke multiple languages, so they were valuable assets to the Corps of Discovery.

Sacagawea did more than translate. She negotiated with Native American tribes, navigated through a tricky

1791—THE BILL OF RIGHTS IS RATIFIED.

1797—JOHN ADAMS IS INAUGURATED AS THE SECOND PRESIDENT OF THE UNITED STATES.

mountain pass, and identified the plants, roots, and berries that were safe to use as food and medicine. Sacagawea's presence and communication skills helped keep peace with tribes that understandably viewed the expedition's motives with suspicion. Amazingly, she did all of this while carrying her infant, Jean Baptiste, on her back.

At the conclusion of the expedition, Charbonneau received $500 for his service to the Corps of Discovery, but Sacagawea never received any payment.

Although her hard work went unpaid, Sacagawea is one of the most celebrated women in US history. According to the journal of another trader, in 1812 Sacagawea became ill and passed away at the youthful age of 25. However, some members of her tribe believe based on oral history that she may have left Charbonneau and lived until 1884.

COMING UP: SACAGAWEA WAS USING HER KNOWLEDGE TO HELP THE CORPS OF DISCOVERY IN THE WEST, WHILE LUCRETIA MOTT WAS SPEAKING OUT PASSIONATELY AGAINST SLAVERY AND GENDER DISCRIMINATION, OR UNFAIR TREATMENT, IN THE EASTERN UNITED STATES.

1799—GEORGE WASHINGTON DIES.

1801—THOMAS JEFFERSON IS INAUGURATED AS THE THIRD PRESIDENT OF THE UNITED STATES.

LUCRETIA MOTT
(1793-1880)

FEMINIST ACTIVIST AND ADVOCATE
FOR ENDING SLAVERY

Women who dared to speak out politically during the 19th century were sharply criticized. But this didn't stop Lucretia Mott from sharing her beliefs that slavery should end and women should be treated fairly.

Lucretia was born in 1793 to a ship captain and his wife. Active members of the Society of Friends, or **Quakers**, the family believed that all people were of equal value and worth. This belief grew stronger as Lucretia grew up and learned of the horrors of slavery and had first-hand experience with the unfair treatment of women.

As a young woman, Lucretia married James Mott, a partner in her father's business. He supported and encouraged Lucretia's efforts to speak out against slavery and advocate for equal treatment of women.

Passionate speeches helped Lucretia gain notoriety as an abolitionist. She traveled all over the northeastern United States speaking to audiences about the evils of slavery, even gaining a personal audience with President John Tyler.

Lucretia did not just speak about the insidiousness of slavery. She also consciously avoided goods created using enslaved labor, like sugar and cotton. When hosting birthday parties for her children, Lucretia used alternative

WOMEN living in 19th-century America had little protection under existing law. Women could not vote, attend college, or enter most professions. When a woman did work, she was paid a fraction of what a man earned. Once married, a woman forfeited all property to her husband, and he had complete legal power over her.

1803—THE LOUISIANA PURCHASE IS MADE.

1804—THE LEWIS AND CLARK EXPEDITION BEGINS TO EXPLORE AND MAP THE LAND CONTAINED IN THE LOUISIANA PURCHASE.

sweeteners to make treats. She attached the following verse to bags of treats: "Take this, my friend, you need not fear to eat. No slave hath toiled to cultivate this sweet."

In addition to her desire to end slavery, Lucretia fought for equality for women and often delivered speeches in which the rights of women and enslaved people were intertwined. In 1848, Lucretia and other like-minded women organized the Seneca Falls Convention, where they demanded rights for American women, including voting, custody, and property rights.

COMING UP: LUCRETIA MOTT TRAVELED FAR AND WIDE DELIVERING ANTI-SLAVERY AND PRO-WOMEN'S RIGHTS SPEECHES. SHE WASN'T ALONE IN THE EFFORT TO SECURE EQUALITY FOR ALL PEOPLE; SOJOURNER TRUTH SHARED LUCRETIA'S PASSION FOR EQUALITY.

1807—THE STEAMBOAT IS INVENTED.

1809—JAMES MADISON IS INAUGURATED AS THE FOURTH PRESIDENT OF THE UNITED STATES.

SOJOURNER TRUTH
(CA. 1797-1883)

AFRICAN AMERICAN ABOLITIONIST
AND WOMEN'S RIGHTS ACTIVIST

Refusing to allow the circumstances of her life to stand in her way, Sojourner Truth influenced many with her outspoken stance on ending slavery and securing women's rights.

Sojourner was born into slavery in present-day New York in 1797 under the name Isabella. Sadly, she was taken from her family around age nine, and after being sold and purchased several times, she was taken to the Dumont family's farm in New York. Like many enslaved individuals, she was abused and forced to work long hours.

Sojourner married an enslaved man, Thomas, and had five children. The state of New York **emancipated** all enslaved people on July 4, 1827. However, the Dumont family claimed Sojourner owed them extra work and refused to grant her full emancipation.

AFRICAN AMERICAN men serving in the Union Army during the Civil War faced extraordinary challenges. They received less pay than white soldiers and had less access to medical care. If captured by the Confederate Army, African American soldiers were handled violently and faced more risk than their white counterparts.

With her infant daughter Sophia in her arms, Sojourner escaped from her owners and sought refuge with a nearby abolitionist family. The family was kind to Sojourner, paying to secure her freedom and helping with the legal battle to have Sojourner's son Peter returned to her after he was illegally sold into slavery in Alabama.

1812–THE UNITED STATES AGAIN BATTLES ENGLAND DURING THE WAR OF 1812.

1814–FRANCIS SCOTT KEY WRITES "THE STAR-SPANGLED BANNER" DURING THE BOMBARDMENT OF FORT MCHENRY. THE WAR OF 1812 ENDS.

Later, Sojourner began to speak about the need for racial and gender equality. In 1851, Sojourner delivered a famous speech at the Women's Rights Convention in Ohio, later referred to as "Ain't I a Woman?" During this speech, she contrasted how society said women were delicate and should be protected by men with how she had been treated in her life. Although she was illiterate, she wrote a book, *The Narrative of Sojourner Truth,* with the help of an assistant.

Sojourner used her influence to gain food and clothing donations for volunteer regiments of black Union soldiers during the Civil War. She participated in efforts to improve the lives of formerly enslaved people for the remainder of her life. Sojourner passed away in Michigan around the age of 92.

COMING UP: WHILE SOJOURNER TRUTH ADVOCATED FOR THE RIGHTS OF WOMEN AND THE END OF SLAVERY, DOROTHEA DIX DID EVERYTHING IN HER POWER TO IMPROVE CONDITIONS FOR THE POOR AND MENTALLY ILL.

1817—JAMES MONROE IS INAUGURATED AS THE FIFTH PRESIDENT OF THE UNITED STATES.

1818—THE FLAG OF THE UNITED STATES IS ADOPTED BY CONGRESS AND CONTAINS 20 STARS, ONE FOR EACH STATE AT THE TIME.

DOROTHEA DIX
(1802-1887)

ADVOCATE FOR THE POOR AND MENTALLY ILL

The 19th century was unkind to the mentally ill and poor. Struggling people were often placed in jails or in **almshouses**, in uncomfortable, sometimes **inhumane**, conditions. Dorothea Dix saw the injustices facing this part of society and vowed to make changes.

Dorothea Dix was born into an unhappy, neglectful home in 1802. She left her parents' home and moved in with her wealthy grandmother around age 12. With the support of her grandmother, Dorothea completed her education and founded an elementary school.

Through personal experience, Dorothea developed compassion for individuals facing mental illness and poverty. When visiting a women's jail to teach a class, she noticed that mentally ill women were neglected. Moved by this experience, Dorothea penned a written request to the Massachusetts legislature asking for money to establish a treatment facility for the mentally ill. She went on to tour facilities where mentally ill individuals were housed in several other states to help others understand their plight.

INDIVIDUALS with mental illness were often placed in jails, asylums, or other buildings meant to contain and keep them away from the rest of society. The mentally ill people living in these situations received little medical care or treatment. Instead, they were placed in painful restraints or even cages.

In addition to her social activism, Dorothea contributed to the Union cause during the Civil War. She was appointed to the role of Superintendent of Army Nurses, working tirelessly to recruit the best nurses and improve the training they received.

1820—THE MISSOURI COMPROMISE PASSES IN CONGRESS, ALLOWING SLAVERY IN THE MISSOURI TERRITORY BUT PROHIBITING IT IN OTHER STATES NORTH OF THE 36°30' PARALLEL.

1825—THE ERIE CANAL IS COMPLETED.

Once the Civil War ended, Dorothea continued to advocate for better care for people with mental illnesses. Her influence helped change the practice of treating mentally ill individuals both in the United States and in other countries.

COMING UP: DOROTHEA DIX WORKED TIRELESSLY TO DRAW ATTENTION TO THE TREATMENT OF MENTALLY ILL INDIVIDUALS, WHILE HARRIET BEECHER STOWE WROTE A COMPELLING ANTI-SLAVERY NOVEL.

1826–JOHN ADAMS AND THOMAS JEFFERSON DIE ON THE SAME DAY, EXACTLY 50 YEARS AFTER THE ADOPTION OF THE DECLARATION OF INDEPENDENCE.

1829–ANDREW JACKSON IS INAUGURATED AS THE SEVENTH PRESIDENT OF THE UNITED STATES.

HARRIET BEECHER STOWE
(1811-1896)
ABOLITIONIST AND AUTHOR

Dedicated to ending the brutality of slavery in the United States, Harriet Beecher Stowe used her talent for writing to change our nation's attitude toward slavery.

Born to a minister and his wife in 1811, Harriet was one of 13 children. Her mother passed away when Harriet was only five years old.

From an early age, Harriet exhibited a gift for writing. Her early books and articles covered a variety of topics, like the American West, religion, and homemaking.

Her marriage to Calvin Stowe in 1836 did not dampen her passion for writing. While raising seven children, Harriet continued to write.

In the midst of a dreadful **cholera** epidemic, Harriet lost a young son. She compared her tragedy to the devastation enslaved mothers experienced when their children were sold away from them.

UNCLE TOM'S CABIN was translated into multiple languages and even performed as a play. Today, many people find the characters in *Uncle Tom's Cabin* to be stereotypical but in Harriet's day, this novel was a groundbreaking plea to put an end to slavery.

Soon after Harriet lost her son, the Fugitive Slave Act of 1850 was signed into law, legally requiring citizens to return enslaved individuals who had sought refuge in the more tolerant Northern states from slavery in the South. This law sparked outrage and led Harriet to write the book she is best known for, *Uncle Tom's Cabin*. Although the novel was written using fictional enslaved characters,

1831—NAT TURNER, AN ENSLAVED MAN, LEADS A SLAVE REBELLION, KILLING AT LEAST 55 WHITE CITIZENS IN VIRGINIA.

1833—OBERLIN COLLEGE BECOMES THE FIRST COEDUCATIONAL COLLEGE IN THE UNITED STATES.

Harriet used her observations of slavery and the firsthand experiences of others to write the book. *Uncle Tom's Cabin* highlighted the glaring differences between the North and South that led to the Civil War, and it was instrumental in the abolitionist movement.

During the final decades of her life, Harriet was involved in the launching of the Hartford Art School, part of the present-day University of Hartford in Connecticut.

COMING UP: HARRIET BEECHER STOWE AND ELIZABETH CADY STANTON BOTH USED WRITING TO FIGHT AGAINST INEQUALITY. WHILE HARRIET WROTE PASSIONATELY FOR ABOLITION, ELIZABETH WROTE FIERCELY FOR WOMEN'S RIGHT TO VOTE.

1836—THE BATTLE OF THE ALAMO OCCURS DURING THE TEXAS REVOLUTION.

1838—THE CHEROKEE ARE FORCED BY THE GOVERNMENT TO LEAVE THEIR HOMELAND AND WALK 1,000 MILES TO WHAT WOULD LATER BECOME OKLAHOMA; OVER 4,000 DIE ON THE "TRAIL OF TEARS."

ELIZABETH CADY STANTON
(1815-1902)
SUFFRAGIST

The right to vote is something that many people take for granted today. However, for Elizabeth Cady Stanton and other women living in the 19th century, **disenfranchisement** was their reality. Committed to obtaining equal status and protections for women, Elizabeth dedicated much of her time to writing, delivering speeches, and advocacy.

Born in 1815 to a well-known lawyer and his wife, Elizabeth, unlike most women of her day, received a formal education. She spent time in her father's library and learned that women were viewed as less than men in the eyes of the law. Once married, husbands controlled the property, wages, and status of their wives.

In 1840, Elizabeth married Henry Stanton, an influential abolitionist, and joined the anti-slavery movement. When the couple attended the World Anti-Slavery Convention in London, England, Elizabeth was upset to find out that women were not allowed to participate as delegates. At the convention, she met another **activist**, or advocate for a cause, Lucretia Mott, who also disagreed with the exclusion of women from the assembly.

Years later, back in the United States, Elizabeth, Lucretia, and others organized the Seneca Falls Convention in New York. The purpose of this meeting was to declare support for women's rights. This convention is considered the birth of the women's **suffrage** movement, an effort to secure the right to vote. Elizabeth was the main author of the Declaration of Sentiments, which was presented at

1841–FOLLOWING THE DEATH OF PRESIDENT WILLIAM HENRY HARRISON, JOHN TYLER BECOMES THE FIRST VICE PRESIDENT TO ASSUME THE PRESIDENCY OF THE UNITED STATES.

1845–*NARRATIVE OF THE LIFE OF FREDERICK DOUGLASS* IS PUBLISHED, FUELING THE ABOLITIONIST MOVEMENT.

the convention. Modeled on the Declaration of Independence, it demanded equality for women under the law.

Elizabeth served as president of the National Woman Suffrage Association for 21 years, but she did not live to see American women gain suffrage. She died 18 years before the Nineteenth Amendment to the Constitution granted women the right to vote.

UNTIL 1920, women were barred from voting. Gaining the right to vote took decades of hard work from several generations of American women. Women fighting for suffrage marched, delivered speeches, wrote, and held parades to gain support. They faced arrest, jail, and abuse from people who disagreed with women's suffrage.

COMING UP: ELIZABETH CADY STANTON AND SUSAN B. ANTHONY WERE FRIENDS WITH THE SAME GOALS IN MIND: INCREASING RIGHTS FOR WOMEN AND SECURING THE RIGHT TO VOTE.

1845—THE REPUBLIC OF TEXAS IS ANNEXED AND BECOMES THE 28TH US STATE.

1846—THE MEXICAN-AMERICAN WAR BEGINS.

SUSAN B. ANTHONY
(1820-1906)

WOMEN'S RIGHTS ACTIVIST AND SOCIAL REFORMER

Equal rights for women wasn't the only cause Susan B. Anthony championed. She was an outspoken abolitionist who worked to improve the lives of African Americans. Susan advocated for black children to be admitted to public schools and helped those escaping slavery as a participant in the Underground Railroad.

Susan was born into a Quaker family in 1820. Her parents, firm in the belief that all men and women were equal under God, were committed to improving society and ending slavery, even opening the family farm to abolitionist meetings. Her father insisted that each of his seven children, girls as well as boys, receive a proper education.

After serving as a teacher for many years, Susan decided to leave the profession and devote herself to social causes. Defying the expectation that women remain silent on social issues, Susan delivered public speeches condemning slavery.

THE EDUCATION of 19th-century girls was largely dependent on the social class to which their families belonged. Wealthier families could pay for attendance at private academies or hire an instructor to teach their daughters. Girls from middle-class or poor families were sometimes allowed to attend their town's school, but only on a limited basis.

Later, Susan met Elizabeth Cady Stanton and the two women formed a partnership, working together to promote women's rights. While Elizabeth, home with her seven children, authored speeches and texts, Susan traveled the country collecting signatures on petitions, delivering speeches, and encouraging other women to organize rights groups. Together, Susan and Elizabeth

1848—LED BY LUCRETIA MOTT AND ELIZABETH CADY STANTON, THE SENECA FALLS CONVENTION, THE FIRST AMERICAN WOMEN'S RIGHTS CONVENTION, IS HELD IN SENECA FALLS, NEW YORK.

1848—THE CALIFORNIA GOLD RUSH BEGINS.

published a weekly paper called *The Revolution* with the following motto: "Men, their rights and nothing more; women, their rights and nothing less."

Susan staged her own protest by voting in the 1872 presidential election. She was arrested and found guilty at trial. Her punishment was a fine of $100, which she refused to pay.

Although Susan died 14 years before women were given the right to vote, she is remembered today as the face of the women's suffrage movement.

COMING UP: WHILE SUSAN B. ANTHONY CHAMPIONED EQUAL RIGHTS, HARRIET TUBMAN RISKED LIFE AND LIMB TO HELP PEOPLE ESCAPE SLAVERY.

1850–THE FUGITIVE SLAVE ACT IS PASSED BY CONGRESS.

1852–*UNCLE TOM'S CABIN* IS PUBLISHED.

HARRIET TUBMAN
(CA. 1820-1913)

AFRICAN AMERICAN ABOLITIONIST AND POLITICAL ACTIVIST; RESCUED ENSLAVED PEOPLE USING THE UNDERGROUND RAILROAD

Attempting to escape from slavery was a risky endeavor. Harriet Tubman not only secured her own freedom, she also helped many enslaved individuals reach freedom in the North. Her bravery and heart made her one of the most celebrated women of the Civil War era.

Harriet Tubman was born in 1820 to enslaved parents on a plantation in Maryland. She was often sent to work for other slave owners, so she learned a great deal about nature, water travel, **constellations**, and the secret networks enslaved communities used to pass messages.

As a young teenager, Harriet received a devastating blow to the head when she tried to help an enslaved friend who was in trouble. Because of this injury, she experienced headaches, seizures, and hallucinations for the rest of her life.

THE UNDERGROUND RAILROAD was a secret network of people who helped enslaved individuals escape from the South. Ushering escapees to freedom was risky, so people involved in the Underground Railroad used code words, symbols, and even constellations to help escapees find safety and resources.

When Harriet was around 29 years old, her owner suddenly died and she was in danger of being sold. So, with all of the courage she could muster, Harriet escaped from slavery with the help of abolitionists along the Underground Railroad.

Once Harriet reached freedom in Philadelphia, she established a new life. Months later, however, she learned that her children and another family member were going

1853–THE GADSDEN PURCHASE ADDS PORTIONS OF WHAT WOULD BECOME ARIZONA AND NEW MEXICO TO THE UNITED STATES.

1857–IN THE DRED SCOTT DECISION, THE SUPREME COURT RULES THAT AN ENSLAVED PERSON DOES NOT BECOME FREE SIMPLY BECAUSE THEY ARE TRANSPORTED INTO A FREE STATE.

to be sold. Harriet carefully and quietly traveled back to Maryland and led her loved ones to freedom.

Despite ever-present danger, Harriet Tubman ushered more than 70 enslaved individuals to freedom. Later in life, she proudly told people that she never lost a passenger on the Underground Railroad.

At the conclusion of the Civil War, when there were no more enslaved men and women to rescue, Harriet devoted herself to women's suffrage, or securing the right to vote for American women. Additionally, she founded a home for elderly African Americans and resided there until her death in 1913.

COMING UP: LIVING AND WORKING IN THE SAME ERA, BOTH HARRIET TUBMAN AND CLARA BARTON HELPED PEOPLE IN NEED.

1859—THE ABOLITIONIST RAID LED BY JOHN BROWN ON HARPERS FERRY FUELS TENSION BETWEEN THE NORTH AND SOUTH.

1860—THE PONY EXPRESS IS FOUNDED.

CLARA BARTON

(1821-1912)

NURSE IN THE CIVIL WAR; FOUNDER
OF THE AMERICAN RED CROSS

Lovingly nicknamed "the angel of the battlefield," Clara Barton worked tirelessly to help wounded soldiers on the front lines of the Civil War. Later, she founded the American Red Cross, a humanitarian organization.

Clara Barton, born in 1821, began her life of service as a child. When her brother sustained a serious injury, Clara spent two years administering his medications, even applying **leeches**, as recommended by the family's doctor.

Clara worked as a teacher and then as a copyist and recording clerk at the United States Patent Office in

Washington, DC. However, when the Civil War broke out in 1861, Clara committed herself to helping Union soldiers in need.

Clara joined other women in collecting medical supplies for Civil War soldiers, but she wanted to do more. So she risked her own safety to deliver supplies to desperate surgeons trying to save as many wounded soldiers as possible. Later, Clara was granted permission to help the wounded on the front lines and could be seen morning to night delivering water as well as feeding, comforting, and tending to injured soldiers.

ALTHOUGH Civil War doctors did the best they could with limited training and supplies and few nurses, disease ran rampant through Civil War camps. More soldiers died from disease than died in battle. Little was known about the spread of disease during the 1860s, so thousands of soldiers were lost to preventable illnesses.

1860—SOUTH CAROLINA BECOMES THE FIRST STATE TO SECEDE FROM THE UNION.

1861—IN MARCH, ABRAHAM LINCOLN IS INAUGURATED AS THE 16TH PRESIDENT OF THE UNITED STATES.

1861—IN APRIL, CONFEDERATE FORCES FIRE ON FORT SUMTER, BEGINNING THE CIVIL WAR.

At the conclusion of the Civil War, Clara assisted in the effort to mark the graves of fallen soldiers and investigated the fates of those who remained missing. Later, while traveling through Europe, Clara heard about the International Red Cross. Upon her return to the United States, she founded an American version of the organization in 1881. She served as president of the American Red Cross for the next 23 years.

COMING UP: BOTH CLARA BARTON AND ELIZABETH BLACKWELL DID THEIR PARTS TO HELP WOMEN ADVANCE IN THE FIELD OF MEDICINE.

1861—IN JULY, CONFEDERATE FORCES DEFEAT UNION FORCES DURING THE FIRST BATTLE OF BULL RUN.

1862—PRESIDENT ABRAHAM LINCOLN DELIVERS THE EMANCIPATION PRO-CLAMATION, WHICH IN JANUARY 1863 FREES ALL SLAVES IN CONFEDERATE STATES.

ELIZABETH
BLACKWELL
(1821–1910)

FIRST WOMAN TO RECEIVE A MEDICAL DEGREE IN THE UNITED STATES

When Elizabeth Blackwell was born, there were no credentialed female doctors in the United States. Overcoming rejection and discrimination, Elizabeth became the first woman awarded the doctor of medicine, or MD, degree in the United States.

Elizabeth was born in England in 1821 to Quaker parents, Samuel and Hannah Blackwell. The family immigrated to Ohio when Elizabeth was around 11 years old. Six years later, her father died, so Elizabeth, her mother, and sisters went to work in the teaching profession.

Elizabeth visited a dying family friend who suggested that she may have been spared some pain if her doctor had been a woman. Because of this interaction, Elizabeth was inspired to pursue a medical degree.

IN 1857, Dr. Elizabeth Blackwell, along with her sister, Dr. Emily Blackwell, opened the New York Infirmary for Women and Children. Soon after, Elizabeth moved on and left Emily to manage the facility for 40 years. Emily built the infirmary into a bustling center of medicine, serving thousands of patients per year.

After many letters of rejection, she was accepted to the Geneva Medical College in the state of New York. The school faculty had given the all-male student body the chance to vote on admitting a woman. Thinking it was a joke, the students voted yes. Elizabeth quickly proved her aptitude for medicine. She graduated at the top of her class with an MD degree in 1849.

In 1857, with the help of her physician sister, Emily, Elizabeth founded the New York **Infirmary** for Women

1863—IN THE BATTLE OF GETTYSBURG, UNION FORCES DEFEAT CONFEDERATE FORCES IN THE BLOODIEST BATTLE OF THE WAR.

1865—IN APRIL, THE CIVIL WAR ENDS WITH THE SURRENDER OF CONFEDERATE TROOPS. PRESIDENT ABRAHAM LINCOLN IS ASSASSINATED A FEW DAYS LATER.

and Children. A decade later, Elizabeth opened a medical college near the infirmary where aspiring female physicians could learn, and where poor patients could receive medical care.

After founding the infirmary and medical college, Elizabeth returned to England and served as a professor at a medical school for women. She wrote books and continued to be involved in promoting better opportunities for women in medicine until her death in 1910.

COMING UP: WHILE ELIZABETH BLACKWELL WAS BLAZING A TRAIL FOR FEMALE PHYSICIANS, MARY HARRIS "MOTHER" JONES WAS ORGANIZING LABORERS TO DEMAND BETTER PAY AND WORKING CONDITIONS.

1865—IN APRIL, VICE PRESIDENT ANDREW JOHNSON BECOMES PRESIDENT OF THE UNITED STATES FOLLOWING LINCOLN'S ASSASSINATION.

1865—IN DECEMBER, THE THIRTEENTH AMENDMENT IS RATIFIED, OUTLAWING SLAVERY THROUGHOUT THE UNITED STATES.

MARY HARRIS "MOTHER" JONES
(1837-1930)
ORGANIZED LABOR REPRESENTATIVE

Mary Harris Jones, known as Mother Jones, was once dubbed "the most dangerous woman in America" and worked tirelessly for the rights of laborers. Despite being mocked by those in power, she believed that fair wages and treatment for workers were worth the fight.

At five years old, Mary immigrated with her family to Canada, leaving Ireland just before the Irish Potato Famine. Mary was educated in Canada and received training as both a teacher and dressmaker. She worked as a dressmaker in Chicago and later relocated to Tennessee to work as a teacher. It was there that she met and married George Jones, an iron molder and union advocate.

In 1867, an **epidemic** of **yellow fever** took the lives of Mary's husband and children. After this unimaginable tragedy, Mary opened a dressmaking shop in Chicago and sewed for the wealthiest women in the city, all the while noticing the stark contrast between her clients and the working poor who had so little. Sadly, she lost everything due to the Great Chicago Fire of 1871.

After the fire, Mary began to travel from town to town to support the efforts of workers to organize and fight for better treatment. She helped miners, steelworkers, and

THE GREAT CHICAGO FIRE of 1871 was one of the most famous fires in the history of the United States. Beginning in a barn, the fire destroyed more than 17,000 buildings and took the lives of approximately 300 Chicago citizens. About one-third of the city was destroyed and nearly 100,000 people were left homeless.

1868—IN MARCH, PRESIDENT ANDREW JOHNSON IS THE FIRST US PRESIDENT TO BE IMPEACHED.

1869—IN MARCH, ULYSSES S. GRANT, FORMER UNION GENERAL, IS INAUGURATED AS THE 18TH PRESIDENT OF THE UNITED STATES.

textile workers form unions. Because of her actions, she was frequently jailed and even placed on house arrest. Leading and participating in hundreds of labor strikes earned her the nickname "Mother Jones," because she was beloved by so many.

Mary was frustrated with the demands placed on child workers, who were often forced to spend 60 hours per week laboring in factories. In 1903, Mary led child workers on a march from Philadelphia to New York City to show the rich factory owners that they wouldn't put up with this poor treatment any longer.

Today, Mary is remembered for helping workers organize into unions, leading the fight for fair wages and treatment, and her ability to unite workers of different races in an era of discrimination.

COMING UP: MARY HARRIS "MOTHER" JONES WORKED TO IMPROVE CONDITIONS FOR WORKERS, WHILE VICTORIA WOODHULL ADVOCATED FOR WOMEN'S RIGHTS, OPENED A BROKERAGE FIRM ON WALL STREET, AND RAN FOR PRESIDENT.

1869—THE FIRST TRANSCONTINENTAL RAILROAD IS COMPLETED.

1870—THE FIFTEENTH AMENDMENT TO THE CONSTITUTION GIVES AFRICAN AMERICAN MEN THE RIGHT TO VOTE.

VICTORIA WOODHULL
(1838-1927)

FIRST WOMAN TO OWN A BROKERAGE FIRM ON WALL STREET; RAN FOR PRESIDENT OF THE UNITED STATES

Far ahead of her time, Victoria Woodhull made a name for herself as a women's rights activist, leader in the women's suffrage movement, and the first woman to run for president of the United States.

Victoria's upbringing was far from normal. Born in 1838 to an impoverished con man and his wife, Victoria traveled with her family from town to town with their medicine show. Medicine shows were made up of entertainment, like psychic readings and magic tricks, along with attempts to sell special concoctions that allegedly cured diseases, ailments, aches, and pains. Victoria escaped her violent father and married a medicine salesman and self-proclaimed doctor, Canning Woodhull. The marriage was unhappy, and the couple divorced after 11 years.

WALL STREET is the home of the New York Stock Exchange, established in 1792 to create a system for trading financial assets. Although their firm lasted only a few years, Victoria Woodhull and her sister challenged the long-held belief that women were incapable of working in the finance industry.

To support themselves, Victoria and her sister Tennessee Claflin, known as Tennie, established themselves as mediums, or psychics. The sisters moved frequently to avoid being prosecuted for scamming clients.

In New York City, Victoria and her sister became spiritual advisors to wealthy widower Cornelius Vanderbilt. Vanderbilt gave the sisters money to invest

1871—THE GREAT CHICAGO FIRE DESTROYS THOUSANDS OF BUILDINGS, KILLS APPROXIMATELY 300 PEOPLE, AND LEAVES MORE THAN 100,000 HOMELESS.

1872—YELLOWSTONE NATIONAL PARK IS CREATED.

in the stock market, and soon after, they opened the first female-owned brokerage firm on Wall Street in 1870.

Victoria and Tennie then founded a newspaper and used the weekly publication as a platform to promote equality in the workplace for women and encourage women's suffrage. They also used the newspaper for a surprising announcement: Victoria was running for president of the United States. The excitement was short-lived, however, because a controversial story in their paper soon led to Victoria's arrest. She spent election day in jail.

In 1877, Victoria and her sister left the United States to settle in England. Continuing to participate in social causes for the remainder of her life, Victoria died at the age of 88. She is remembered today as a trailblazer for women's rights.

COMING UP: WHILE VICTORIA WOODHULL HOPED TO BECOME THE FIRST FEMALE PRESIDENT OF THE UNITED STATES, QUEEN LILI'UOKALANI FOUGHT TO RETAIN HER RIGHT TO THE HAWAIIAN THRONE.

1876—IN FEBRUARY, THE NATIONAL LEAGUE OF BASEBALL, THE FIRST OF THE MAJOR LEAGUES, IS FOUNDED.

1876—IN JUNE, ALLIED LAKOTA, NORTHERN CHEYENNE, AND ARAPAHO TRIBES DEFEAT US FORCES IN THE BATTLE OF THE LITTLE BIGHORN.

QUEEN LILI'UOKALANI
(1838-1917)

LAST MONARCH OF THE KINGDOM OF HAWAI'I

Hawaii joined the United States in 1959 as the 50th state in the union, despite the objections of scores of native Hawaiians. Queen Lili'uokalani, the final Hawaiian ruler, struggled to protect Hawaiians in the face of strong opposition.

Born in 1838, Lili'uokalani was a talented musician and songwriter. Years of involvement in the Hawaiian government prepared her to become queen of the Kingdom of Hawai'i in 1891.

Queen Lili'uokalani's rule faced challenges. A change in US law affected the sugar industry in Hawai'i. Hawaiian sugar was now considered a foreign product, and the costs to import sugar to the United States increased. The Hawaiian sugar industry was near ruin.

On top of sugar industry frustrations, Queen Lili'uokalani's power was limited due to a new restrictive constitution. After an unsuccessful attempt to change the constitution, an angry group of American businessmen and military members staged a **coup**.

Faced with few choices, Queen Lili'uokalani surrendered to the militia in an effort to avoid loss of life. She was confident that the US government would restore her to the throne of Hawai'i once all of the facts were known.

HAWAII became the 50th state on August 21, 1959. However, for many native Hawaiians, this is not a date to celebrate. Hawaii's statehood status has been surrounded by controversy from the very beginning. Hawaii's past as an independent nation leads many to question whether the addition of this island state was fair to its native inhabitants.

1879—THOMAS EDISON INVENTS THE FIRST COMMERCIALLY PRACTICAL LIGHT BULB.

1880—THE POPULATION OF THE UNITED STATES EXCEEDS 50 MILLION.

In an attempt to restore Queen Liliʻuokalani to the throne, there was an unsuccessful revolt. Upon the discovery of hidden weapons, Liliʻuokalani was put on trial for treason and subsequently placed on house arrest in ʻIolani Palace.

Queen Liliʻuokalani had no biological children, so she chose an heir, her niece Kaʻiulani. Both women traveled to Washington, DC, to talk with government leaders in an attempt to restore the Hawaiian **monarchy**. Their pleas were ignored.

Sadly, Queen Liliʻuokalani died in exile at the age of 79. Her dream of a free Hawaiʻi is still active today. Descendants of former Hawaiian rulers continue to claim the throne and advocate for an independent Hawaiʻi.

COMING UP: WHILE QUEEN LILIʻUOKALANI WORKED TO RETAIN HER RIGHT TO THE HAWAIIAN THRONE, FRANCES WILLARD WAS ACTIVE IN THE WOMEN'S SUFFRAGE MOVEMENT WHILE CONTRIBUTING TO OTHER CAUSES, LIKE WOMEN'S HIGHER EDUCATION AND SOCIAL REFORMS.

1882—THE CHINESE EXCLUSION ACT PROHIBITS ALL IMMIGRATION OF CHINESE LABORERS.

1885—THE WASHINGTON MONUMENT IN WASHINGTON, DC, IS COMPLETED.

FRANCES WILLARD
(1839-1898)

PRESIDENT OF WOMAN'S CHRISTIAN TEMPERANCE
UNION; ADVOCATE FOR SUFFRAGE AND THE HIGHER
EDUCATION OF WOMEN

As a teacher, lecturer, and leader, Frances Willard worked to encourage reforms in many areas of society, including women's rights, **temperance**, and education.

Born in 1839, Frances was educated mostly at home by her mother. However, she did attend a one-room school for a short time and later attended a college for women. Frances worked as a teacher for several years and became president of the Evanston College for Ladies. After two years, she resigned to work in the women's temperance movement, or the movement to encourage people to reduce or end their alcohol consumption.

Frances helped establish the Woman's Christian Temperance Union (WCTU) in 1874 and served as the organization's president beginning in 1879. Under Frances's leadership, the WCTU worked to empower women and help them learn the skills needed to be productive members of society. Frances traveled extensively throughout the United States giving lectures, distributing petitions, and teaching women to organize social reform groups.

Although reducing the consumption of alcohol was at the center of the WCTU, Frances expanded the group's focus to include suffrage, women's rights, and more

THE WCTU was founded in 1874 by women hoping to end the consumption of alcohol in their communities. Women were frustrated because they had no legal recourse against the negative behavior caused by alcohol consumption. The WCTU is still active today and advocates the prevention of alcohol, drug, and tobacco use.

1885—GROVER CLEVELAND IS INAUGURATED AS THE 22ND PRESIDENT OF THE UNITED STATES.

1886—THE STATUE OF LIBERTY IS DEDICATED IN NEW YORK HARBOR BY PRESIDENT GROVER CLEVELAND.

educational opportunities for women. Additionally, the organization advocated for better conditions for prisoners and for temperance education in schools. Frances believed that it was important for women to seek opportunities to participate in politics and advocate for important causes.

The WCTU flourished under Frances's leadership, growing to 150,000 members, including men sympathetic to the vision of the organization. Frances struggled with her health and died suddenly at the age of 58. To honor her legacy, a statue of Frances Willard was placed in the US Capitol's Statuary Hall.

COMING UP: LIKE FRANCES WILLARD, JANE ADDAMS ADVOCATED FOR WOMEN'S SUFFRAGE IN ADDITION TO CHAMPIONING OTHER SOCIAL CAUSES.

1889–PRESIDENT BENJAMIN HARRISON IS THE EARLIEST US PRESIDENT TO HAVE HIS VOICE RECORDED AND PRESERVED.

1889–THE FIRST OF THE OKLAHOMA LAND RUNS OCCURS, DURING WHICH WHITE SETTLERS RUSH IN TO CLAIM LAND FORMERLY DESIGNATED AS INDIAN TERRITORY.

JANE ADDAMS
(1860-1935)

SOCIAL REFORMER AND ACTIVIST; FIRST AMERICAN WOMAN TO WIN THE NOBEL PEACE PRIZE

Known for her devotion to civic responsibility, Jane Addams was involved in important social changes throughout the United States. Later, her work to encourage peace led to her being the first American woman to be awarded the Nobel Peace Prize.

Born in 1860, Jane was the eighth of nine children. Sadly, her mother died when Jane was only two years old. Even without her mother, Jane lived a privileged life as the daughter of a wealthy mill owner.

While touring London with a friend, Ellen Starr, Jane was impressed with a settlement house that provided services to the families of impoverished factory workers. Upon returning to Chicago, Jane and Ellen leased a large home and established Hull House.

The young women funded their vision for Hull House by giving speeches, hosting fundraisers, and asking for donations from other wealthy young women. Before long, Hull House was helping thousands of people per week by offering a multitude of services, including activities for children, a swimming pool, a coffeehouse, and more.

In addition to her work at Hull House, Jane supported several important organizations, including the National

ONE OF THE FIRST social settlements in the United States, Hull House, was founded in Chicago in 1889 to serve needy citizens and new immigrants living in the surrounding neighborhoods. Although it started small, Hull House grew to include many buildings, including a kindergarten, gymnasium, job training center, and housing area for children.

1890—IN OCTOBER, YOSEMITE NATIONAL PARK IS CREATED.

1890—IN DECEMBER, US TROOPS COMMIT THE WOUNDED KNEE MASSACRE; SEVERAL HUNDRED LAKOTA DIE, MOSTLY WOMEN AND CHILDREN.

Association for the Advancement of Colored People (NAACP) and the American Civil Liberties Union (ACLU). However, she soon discovered that her true passion in life was ridding the world of war. She delivered speeches and wrote about the need for peace. Ignoring sharp criticism, Jane spoke out against American involvement in World War I. Later, Jane founded and served as president of the Women's International League for Peace and Freedom.

Jane's efforts to promote peace were noticed, and in 1931, she became the first American woman to receive the Nobel Peace Prize. Unfortunately, Jane was too ill to attend the ceremony and died four years later, in 1935.

COMING UP: JANE ADDAMS WAS A CHARTERED MEMBER OF THE NAACP, WHICH IDA B. WELLS HELPED ESTABLISH.

1892–ELLIS ISLAND OPENS IN NEW YORK HARBOR AS THE MAIN EAST COAST IMMIGRATION STATION.

1895–GROVER CLEVELAND IS INAUGURATED AS THE 24TH PRESIDENT OF THE UNITED STATES AND IS THE ONLY US PRESIDENT TO SERVE TWO NON-CONSECUTIVE TERMS IN OFFICE.

IDA B. WELLS
(1862-1931)

AFRICAN AMERICAN JOURNALIST AND EDUCATOR; COFOUNDER OF NAACP

As a teacher, journalist, and social activist, Ida B. Wells shined a spotlight on the unfair treatment of African Americans throughout the Southern United States.

Ida was born into slavery in 1862 in Mississippi just before Abraham Lincoln issued the Emancipation Proclamation. Her family was granted freedom in 1865 when Mississippi, a Confederate state, surrendered to Union forces after the Civil War.

Ida's family viewed education as a way to escape poverty. However, Ida had to withdraw from school at the age of 16 when her parents and a sibling died in a yellow fever outbreak. Ida was left to care for her remaining five siblings, so she persuaded a school administrator to give her a job as a teacher.

After moving to Tennessee to continue her teaching career, Ida encountered a situation that changed her life. Although she'd purchased a first-class ticket for the train, she was ordered by the conductor to move to the car designated for African Americans. She refused and was forcefully removed. Ida filed a lawsuit against the train car company and won. Unfortunately, the case was overturned by a federal court.

Later, three black male acquaintances of hers were defending their grocery store against an attack by angry white men when shots were fired and a white deputy

> **FOUNDED IN 1909** by both black and white leaders, the first mission of the NAACP was to end the lynching of African Americans. The organization is still active today and works to ensure employment equality, voting rights, education, and criminal justice reforms.

1896—THE SUPREME COURT RULES IN THE CASE OF *PLESSY V. FERGUSON* THAT RACIAL SEGREGATION IS LEGAL UNDER THE RULE OF "SEPARATE BUT EQUAL."

1898—THE SPANISH-AMERICAN WAR BEGINS AND ENDS AFTER LESS THAN FOUR MONTHS.

sheriff was killed. The black men were arrested but never went to court because a white mob violently removed them from the jail and **lynched** them.

Ida traveled throughout the South to investigate instances of lynching and violence against black people. Despite threats of violence and even the destruction of her newspaper office, Ida published the results of her investigations in pamphlets and newspapers.

Ida helped found the National Association for the Advancement of Colored People (NAACP) and devoted her life to social causes before passing away in 1931.

COMING UP: A PROMINENT JOURNALIST LIKE IDA B. WELLS, NELLIE BLY WENT TO EXTREME LENGTHS TO EXPOSE THE TREATMENT OF THE MENTALLY ILL.

1900—THE POPULATION OF THE UNITED STATES EXCEEDS 75 MILLION.

1900—IN SEPTEMBER, A GREAT STORM STRIKES GALVESTON, TEXAS, BECOMING THE DEADLIEST NATURAL DISASTER IN US HISTORY.

NELLIE BLY

(1864-1922)

JOURNALIST WHO EXPOSED THE TREATMENT OF THE MENTALLY ILL

Courageous journalist Nellie Bly played a major role in improving conditions for mentally ill individuals with a daring undercover investigation.

In 1864, the wealthy Cochran family of Pennsylvania welcomed a daughter, Elizabeth Jane. Elizabeth grew up to be a journalist, publishing under the pen name "Nellie Bly."

After months of trying to find a job in New York City, Nellie convinced the editors of the *New York World* to give her an extraordinary assignment. She would pretend to be mentally ill to gain admittance to the Women's Lunatic Asylum on Blackwell's Island, an **insane asylum** in New York City, to investigate the treatment of patients.

NELLIE BLY reached celebrity status in the United States when she set a record for the fastest trip around the world on January 25, 1890. Nellie crossed the globe in 72 days using trains, steamships, horses, and donkeys.

She had little trouble securing the label "insane" and being committed to the asylum. While undercover, Nellie took notes on what she saw. Patients were ignored and mostly neglected, forced to take cold baths, and locked in small, wet, pest-infested rooms. Additionally, Nellie noticed that women who lacked English proficiency were often committed due to their inability to defend themselves or explain their actions.

With the help of a lawyer, Nellie was finally released from the asylum and authored a book, *Ten Days in a*

1901—IN SEPTEMBER, VICE PRESIDENT THEODORE ROOSEVELT BECOMES THE 26TH PRESIDENT OF THE UNITED STATES FOLLOWING PRESIDENT WILLIAM MCKINLEY'S ASSASSINATION.

1901—THE FIRST MASS-PRODUCED AUTOMOBILE IS CREATED.

Mad-House. Her story was shared across the nation, and New York City improved the treatment of the mentally ill by providing nutritious meals and better sanitation, and terminating abusive doctors and nurses.

Nellie continued her journalistic career by reporting on World War I and the fight for women's suffrage. At age 31, she married Robert Seaman, a very successful businessman. When he died less than 10 years later, Nellie retired from journalism and managed his company. She died in 1922 at 57 years old.

COMING UP: WHILE JOURNALIST NELLIE BLY WROTE TO EXPOSE THE INHUMANE TREATMENT OF THE MENTALLY ILL, CLARA LEMLICH ORGANIZED EMPLOYEES IN THE NEW YORK GARMENT INDUSTRY AGAINST POOR TREATMENT IN THE WORKPLACE.

1903—IN OCTOBER, THE FIRST WORLD SERIES TAKES PLACE.

1903—IN DECEMBER, THE WRIGHT BROTHERS DEMONSTRATE THE FIRST FLIGHT OF A POWERED AIRCRAFT.

CLARA LEMLICH
(1886-1982)

LEADER OF A STRIKE OF SHIRTWAIST WORKERS IN THE GARMENT INDUSTRY

An outspoken voice in the fight for workers' rights, Clara Lemlich led a strike of 20,000 garment workers.

Clara, born in 1886, faced anti-Jewish discrimination and tough economic conditions in her native Ukraine. Her family, seeking a better life, immigrated to the United States in 1903.

Once in New York City, Clara found work at the Gotham shirtwaist factory. She typically worked 11 hours per day, six days per week, and earned around three dollars per week. Hoping to help improve working conditions, Clara joined the International Ladies' Garment Workers' Union (ILGWU) and soon found herself organizing picket lines and strikes.

In 1909, thousands of garment workers, fed up with low pay and long hours, gathered to discuss a general strike. While listening to speakers discouraging a strike, Clara could not contain her frustration. She ran to the stage and urged the crowd to pledge their participation in a general strike. The massive audience stood, cheered, and voted to strike.

IN 1911, a devastating fire at the Triangle Shirtwaist Factory took the lives of nearly 150 workers, most of them young women. The fire originated near the top of the factory, too high for the firefighters' ladders to reach. Workers were trapped inside because managers had locked the fire escape doors. This tragedy led to reforms in safety regulations for workers.

The next day, over 15,000 garment makers in New York walked out in demand of a 20 percent raise, fewer work hours, and paid overtime. The next day, that number

1906—THE SAN FRANCISCO EARTHQUAKE DESTROYS OVER 80 PERCENT OF THE CITY.

1909—THE ONE-CENT COIN, OR PENNY, ADOPTS A DESIGN FEATURING ABRAHAM LINCOLN.

increased to more than 20,000 workers representing 500 factories who walked out and began picketing.

The strike continued for more than two months, and during that time, many factory owners negotiated with workers. During the next few years, there were many strikes staged by female workers. However, the limited improvements made were not enough to prevent the devastating 1911 Triangle Shirtwaist Fire in New York City.

For the rest of her life, Clara delivered speeches on a variety of causes and continued to advocate for the rights of workers. She even helped the orderlies in her nursing home organize a union before she died in 1982 at 96 years old.

COMING UP: THE EARLY 1900S WERE A TIME FOR WOMEN TO SHINE. CLARA LEMLICH ORGANIZED WORKERS TO FIGHT FOR BETTER CONDITIONS, WHILE HELEN KELLER FOUGHT TO FURTHER THE NEEDS OF INDIVIDUALS WITH DISABILITIES.

1912—IN MARCH, GIRL SCOUTS OF THE UNITED STATES OF AMERICA IS FOUNDED BY JULIETTE GORDON LOW.

1912—IN APRIL, THE RMS *TITANIC* STRIKES AN ICEBERG AND SINKS ON ITS MAIDEN VOYAGE.

HELEN KELLER
(1880-1968)

FIRST PERSON WITH DEAF-BLINDNESS TO EARN A BACHELOR OF ARTS DEGREE; POLITICAL ACTIVIST AND LECTURER

Determined to overcome her health challenges, Helen Keller invested her time and effort into advocating for others with disabilities as well as for women's voting rights and other causes.

Helen, born in 1880, contracted an illness at 19 months of age that left her deaf and blind. Helen did not know how to speak, so she communicated with her family by touching their faces to feel facial expressions. Helen's parents recognized their daughter's intelligence but felt helpless when trying to communicate with her.

A teacher named Anne Sullivan was sent to the Keller home by the Perkins School for the Blind. At first, Helen was a difficult student, but Anne kept trying. She taught Helen to create words by spelling them into her palm. Once Helen understood her teacher's method, she learned quickly.

> **THE ACLU** was founded in 1920 by a small group of citizens, including Helen Keller, who were committed to holding the US government accountable to the Bill of Rights. The ACLU is still active today, and its mission is to protect citizens from government overreach.

Once she had a basic understanding of the alphabet and words, Helen enrolled in the Perkins School where she learned to read Braille and write with a special typewriter. Later, she attended Radcliffe College, graduating with honors in 1904. Her teacher, Anne, was by Helen's side through all of her educational pursuits.

1913—WOODROW WILSON IS INAUGURATED AS THE 28TH PRESIDENT OF THE UNITED STATES.

1914—IN MAY, MOTHER'S DAY IS ESTABLISHED AS A NATIONAL HOLIDAY.

Helen, the first person with deaf-blindness to graduate from college, launched a rich, purposeful career helping other people with deaf-blindness, and also supporting many other important causes. In addition to lecturing in various countries, Helen published books and articles and advocated for women's suffrage and **civil rights**. In 1920, Helen worked with other social activists to found the American Civil Liberties Union (ACLU), an organization dedicated to protecting the rights of Americans.

Helen died in 1968 at 87 years old. Because she was so admired, Helen was laid to rest in the National Cathedral in Washington, DC, with her teacher and lifelong friend, Anne Sullivan.

COMING UP: IN THE LATE 1800s, AMERICAN WOMEN WERE ATTENDING COLLEGE MORE THAN EVER BEFORE. AMONG THESE WOMEN WERE HELEN KELLER AND EMILY GREENE BALCH. ALTHOUGH THEY LIVED IN VASTLY DIFFERENT CIRCUMSTANCES, BOTH WOMEN EARNED COLLEGE DEGREES AND POSITIVELY INFLUENCED THEIR COMMUNITIES.

1914—THE ASSASSINATION OF ARCHDUKE FRANZ FERDINAND SPARKS THE START OF WORLD WAR I IN EUROPE.

1915—THE FIRST-EVER STOP SIGN IS INSTALLED IN DETROIT, MICHIGAN.

EMILY GREENE BALCH
(1867-1961)
ECONOMIST, SOCIOLOGIST, PACIFIST

Living a life of service and accomplishment, Emily Greene Balch worked tirelessly to educate women, support the needy, and promote peace.

Born in 1867 to a well-to-do New England family, Emily was raised by progressive parents who encouraged her to complete her education. After graduating from Bryn Mawr College with honors, Emily studied in France. Upon her return to the United States, she helped establish the Denison House, a Boston settlement house that provided needy residents with facilities, activities, and classes.

Later, Emily accepted a faculty position at Wellesley College, where she taught economics and researched economic issues for the next 22 years. During her tenure, she participated in social reform activities aimed at helping the poor and disadvantaged. She spoke out against racism and prejudice.

ON DECEMBER 7, 1941, Japan launched a devastating attack on Pearl Harbor, a US naval base in Hawaii. The following day, the United States entered World War II, declaring war on Japan. Soon after, Japanese Americans were unfairly viewed with suspicion and forced into internment camps where they were separated from the rest of American society and kept in poor conditions.

At the onset of World War I, Emily turned her attention to the cause of world peace. She tried to convince leaders, including President Woodrow Wilson, to allow the United States to remain neutral in the conflict. Her anti-war statements led to her termination from Wellesley College.

In 1919, Emily took part in the Women's International League for Peace and Freedom (WILPF) and became the

1916—JEANNETTE RANKIN BECOMES THE FIRST WOMAN ELECTED TO CONGRESS.

1917—CONGRESS DECLARES WAR ON GERMANY AND JOINS THE ALLIED POWERS.

organization's secretary-treasurer. The women involved in WILPF promoted peace by trying to improve conditions that caused conflict, like economic differences and social issues.

Emily detested war, but after the human rights threats of Nazi Germany and the Japanese attack on Pearl Harbor in 1941, she recognized that force was sometimes a necessary response. She spent the years of World War II helping Japanese Americans held in internment camps and supporting refugees from Nazi Germany.

In 1946, Emily became the second woman to be awarded the Nobel Peace Prize. True to her character, Emily donated her prize winnings to the women's peace movement. She died in 1961 at 94 years old.

COMING UP: WHILE EMILY GREENE BALCH WAS INSPIRING OTHERS TO WORK TOWARD PEACE, GEORGIA O'KEEFFE INSPIRED CREATIVITY WITH HER GROUNDBREAKING ART.

1919—WORLD WAR I ENDS WITH THE SIGNING OF THE TREATY OF VERSAILLES.

1920—WOMEN ARE GIVEN THE RIGHT TO VOTE IN THE NINETEENTH AMENDMENT TO THE CONSTITUTION.

GEORGIA O'KEEFFE
(1887-1986)

ARTIST

Credited with creating over 2,000 artistic works in her lifetime, Georgia O'Keeffe created popular modernist paintings in an era of male-dominated art.

Born in Wisconsin in 1887, Georgia was fortunate to be part of a family that stressed the importance of education for girls. She attended art school and a teachers college, which allowed her to teach art in several states from 1911 to 1918.

After creating a series of charcoal drawings, Georgia caught the attention of New York gallery owner Alfred Stieglitz. Finding her work enchanting, he placed her drawings in his popular art gallery. In 1918, Alfred convinced Georgia to leave her teaching career to live and paint in New York. They married in 1924.

She produced images that related to where she lived and visited. While she lived in New York City, she painted skyscrapers, city buildings, and skylines. For a change of pace, Georgia began to visit New Mexico so that she could paint in a quiet, less-populated environment. It was during her time in New Mexico that she created some of her most famous paintings, portraying her view of the desert, including land formations, unique plants, and even animal skeletons.

DOLE, formerly the Hawaiian Pineapple Company, offered Georgia O'Keeffe a free trip to Hawaii in 1938. The company assumed she would paint a pineapple for them. Instead, Georgia sent the Dole Company two paintings, a flower and a papaya tree—no pineapples! However, she did later relent and paint a pineapple for the company to use in its advertisements.

1924—THE INDIAN CITIZENSHIP ACT GRANTS CITIZENSHIP TO ALL NATIVE AMERICANS BORN IN THE UNITED STATES.

1927—IN MAY, CHARLES LINDBERGH MAKES THE FIRST SOLO, NONSTOP TRANSATLANTIC FLIGHT.

For the last 20 years of her life, Georgia was unable to create art due to the loss of her sight. Georgia proved to everyone that women could produce remarkable pieces of art.

COMING UP: AS GEORGIA O'KEEFFE WAS DISPROVING GENDER STEREOTYPES IN THE WORLD OF ART, ELEANOR ROOSEVELT WAS REVOLUTIONIZING THE ROLE OF THE AMERICAN FIRST LADY.

1927—IN OCTOBER, THE FIRST MOTION PICTURE WITH SOUND IS RELEASED.

1929—A MAJOR STOCK MARKET CRASH BEGINS THE GREAT DEPRESSION.

ELEANOR ROOSEVELT

(1884–1962)

FIRST LADY AND ACTIVIST

Unlike most first ladies before her, Eleanor Roosevelt was outspoken and politically active. As a civil rights and human rights activist, Eleanor redefined the role of the first lady of the United States.

Eleanor was born into a wealthy, well-known family in New York in 1884. Although she had many advantages, her early life was not easy. Both her mother and father died before Eleanor was 10 years old. Eleanor went to live with her maternal grandmother and was educated by private tutors until she was 15 years old. She then went to a boarding school in London with the encouragement of her aunt.

Upon returning to New York in 1902, Eleanor began teaching immigrant families in a settlement house. Eleanor was soon reintroduced to her distant cousin Franklin Delano Roosevelt. When the couple married in 1905, their most famous attendee was President Theodore Roosevelt, Eleanor's uncle and president of the United States.

IN 1939, members of the Daughters of the American Revolution (DAR) refused to let Marian Anderson, a gifted African American opera singer, perform at Constitution Hall because of her race. Eleanor Roosevelt cancelled her DAR membership and helped arrange a historic concert on the steps of the Lincoln Memorial, where Anderson performed for 75,000 people.

While raising their children, Eleanor served as a supporter and political helpmate to her husband. When Franklin received a devastating diagnosis of **polio** in 1921 and became paralyzed from the waist down, Eleanor

1931—THE EMPIRE STATE BUILDING OPENS IN NEW YORK CITY.

1933—FRANKLIN D. ROOSEVELT IS INAUGURATED AS THE 32ND PRESIDENT OF THE UNITED STATES.

encouraged him to remain active in politics. Eleanor saw her husband through multiple political roles from state senator to governor of New York to president of the United States.

When her husband was inaugurated in 1933, she refused to embrace the role of quiet first lady. Instead, Eleanor became the most outspoken, politically active first lady in history. She wrote articles and books and traveled the country giving speeches while observing Americans' living and working conditions. She held weekly press conferences exclusively with female reporters.

After the death of her husband in 1945, Eleanor served as the US delegate to the United Nations and pushed for human rights. For the remainder of her life, Eleanor advocated for civil rights, gender equality, and human rights.

COMING UP: WHILE ELEANOR ROOSEVELT WAS FURTHERING HUMAN RIGHTS CAUSES, AMELIA EARHART WAS PIONEERING IN THE FIELD OF AVIATION.

1934—THE DUST BOWL BEGINS IN THE AMERICAN PRAIRIES, CAUSING SEVERE DROUGHT AND EROSION THAT FORCES TENS OF THOUSANDS OF FAMILIES TO ABANDON THEIR FARMS AND RELOCATE.

1935—THE FBI IS ESTABLISHED, WITH J. EDGAR HOOVER AS ITS DIRECTOR.

AMELIA EARHART
(1897-1937)

AVIATION PIONEER AND AUTHOR

In the early 1900s, there were few women involved in the field of **aviation,** but Amelia Earhart did not let that dampen her desire to fly. Making history as the first woman to fly a plane across the Atlantic Ocean, Amelia inspired women everywhere.

Amelia was born in Kansas in 1897 but did not stay there long. Her father was a railroad attorney, so the family moved frequently. Amelia attended college for a short time but withdrew to pursue other interests.

While working as a nurse's aide during World War I in a Canadian military hospital, Amelia was introduced to the world of flight. As a passenger, Amelia flew for the first time in 1920 and recalled that as soon as the plane left the ground, she knew she had to learn to fly. Amelia hired a flight instructor and paid for lessons while working as

a telephone clerk and photographer. Amelia flew on her own for the first time in 1921 and bought her own airplane in 1922.

In 1928, publisher George Putnam asked Amelia to be the first woman passenger to cross the Atlantic Ocean in a plane, which made her quite popular in the media. When Amelia authored two books, *20 Hrs. 40 Mins.* and *The Fun of It*, George helped her publish and promote them. George and Amelia married in 1931.

Amelia had many opportunities due to her popularity, including access to money to finance her flight ambitions.

1937—THE GOLDEN GATE BRIDGE IS COMPLETED IN SAN FRANCISCO.

1939—IN APRIL, PRESIDENT FRANKLIN D. ROOSEVELT BECOMES THE FIRST PRESIDENT TO APPEAR ON TELEVISION.

In 1932, she made history as the first woman to pilot a plane across the Atlantic Ocean.

Determined to make history again as the first woman to complete an around-the-world flight, Amelia, along with her navigator, Frederick Noonan, departed from Miami, Florida, in June 1937. Sadly, the pair was lost at sea in July.

COMING UP: AMELIA EARHART MADE HISTORY AS A FEMALE AVIATOR WHILE CLARE BOOTHE LUCE FORGED NEW PATHS FOR WOMEN AS A FRONT-LINE WAR CORRESPONDENT, A US CONGRESSWOMAN, AND AN AMBASSADOR.

1939—IN SEPTEMBER, WORLD WAR II BREAKS OUT IN EUROPE.

1940—THE FIRST MCDONALD'S RESTAURANT IS FOUNDED.

CLARE BOOTHE LUCE
(1903-1987)

FIRST WOMAN APPOINTED TO A MAJOR AMBASSADORIAL POST ABROAD; CONGRESSWOMAN; AUTHOR

As a writer, congresswoman, and ambassador, Clare Boothe Luce forged new paths for American women in journalism and politics.

Clare was born in 1903 in New York City. Her childhood was challenging, especially when her father, a concert violinist, abandoned the family. Clare's mother worked tirelessly to ensure that her daughter received a proper education.

At age 20, Clare married George Brokaw. The couple had one daughter; however, the marriage was unhappy and ended in 1929. Soon after, Clare was hired on at *Vogue* magazine and later *Vanity Fair*, working her way up to managing editor in 1934.

The next year, Clare married magazine publisher Henry Luce. Her writing career began to take off, and during World War II, Clare traveled to Europe to write firsthand accounts of the war.

THE PRESIDENTIAL MEDAL of Freedom is America's highest **civilian** honor. This award, established in 1963 by President John F. Kennedy, honors those who have contributed to the United States or to the world. Recipients of this medal come from all walks of life but have one similarity: They've made a difference in the lives of others.

Using the connections made during her journalism career, Clare ran for Congress and won, making her the first female representative from Connecticut. She served with integrity, advocating for equal rights for all citizens and racial integration in the US military.

When her time in Congress ended, Clare remained active in politics and was appointed ambassador to Italy.

1941–JAPANESE FIGHTER PLANES ATTACK PEARL HARBOR, HAWAII. THE NEXT DAY, THE UNITED STATES DECLARES WAR ON JAPAN, OFFICIALLY ENTERING WORLD WAR II.

1945–IN MAY, GERMANY SURRENDERS, ENDING WORLD WAR II IN EUROPE.

President Ronald Reagan presented Clare with the Presidential Medal of Freedom in 1983. When asked to reflect upon her life's work, Clare responded: "Because I am a woman, I must make unusual efforts to succeed. If I fail, no one will say, 'She doesn't have what it takes.' They will say, 'Women don't have what it takes.'"

COMING UP: WHILE CLARE BOOTHE LUCE WAS SERVING THE UNITED STATES AS A CONGRESSWOMAN AND AMBASSADOR, GRACE HOPPER WAS WORKING ON THE VERY FIRST ELECTRONIC COMPUTER AND SERVING AS A REAR ADMIRAL IN THE US NAVY.

1945—IN AUGUST, THE UNITED STATES DROPS ATOMIC BOMBS ON HIROSHIMA AND NAGASAKI, JAPAN.

1945—IN SEPTEMBER, WORLD WAR II ENDS WITH JAPANESE OFFICIAL SURRENDER.

GRACE HOPPER
(1906-1992)

PIONEER OF COMPUTER PROGRAMMING
AND US NAVY REAR ADMIRAL

A woman ahead of her time, Grace Hopper was one of the very first computer programmers and served the US Navy as a rear admiral.

Grace Hopper was born in 1906 in New York City. As a child, Grace displayed an early talent for engineering when she took objects apart and put them back together. Motivated and determined, Grace earned a master's degree and PhD in mathematics from Yale University.

In 1943, during World War II, Grace left her teaching position at Vassar College to enlist in the Navy Women

Accepted for Voluntary Emergency Service (WAVES). Promoted to the rank of lieutenant, Grace, along with a team, developed an early model electronic computer. One day, frustrated by a mystery computer failure, Grace opened the machine and found that

GRACE helped develop the UNIVAC, the world's first all-electronic digital computer. The UNIVAC recorded information on high-speed magnetic tape, which was an improvement over the punch cards used by earlier computers. This computer was used by NASA to communicate with astronauts during the Apollo moon missions.

a moth had flown into the computer, so she began to use the word "bug" to describe computer errors. We still use this word today!

After World War II, Grace continued to work in the field of computer technology, where she helped create the Universal Automatic Computer (UNIVAC), an electronic and digital computer. She also pioneered work in computer languages and codes. In the mid-1950s, computers were

1946—THE FIRST MASS-PRODUCED TELEVISION SET IS CREATED.

1947—THE COLD WAR BETWEEN THE UNITED STATES AND THE SOVIET UNION BEGINS.

massive pieces of machinery, but Grace predicted that future computers would be desk-sized and people from all walks of life would use them daily.

In 1967, Grace was ordered by the Navy to return to active duty and named the director of the Navy Programming Languages Group. She rose in rank, and by 1985 she was promoted to rear admiral. Later, she received the Defense Distinguished Service Medal, the highest honor for a non-combat veteran.

She continued to work in the field of computer technology until her death in 1992. Grace's achievements were again honored in 2016 when she was posthumously awarded the Presidential Medal of Freedom.

COMING UP: GRACE HOPPER LEFT BEHIND A LEGACY OF COMPUTER INNOVATION AND PROUD NAVAL SERVICE, WHILE RACHEL CARSON OPENED AMERICANS' EYES TO THE NEED TO PROTECT OUR NATURAL WORLD.

1947—IN APRIL, JACKIE ROBINSON BECOMES THE FIRST AFRICAN AMERICAN TO PLAY IN MAJOR LEAGUE BASEBALL (MLB).

1947—IN NOVEMBER, THE POLAROID INSTANT CAMERA IS MANUFACTURED.

RACHEL CARSON
(1907-1964)

MARINE BIOLOGIST; CONSERVATIONIST; AUTHOR

Firm in her belief that all living things are connected, Rachel Carson wrote about the natural world and emphasized that people are connected to the ecosystem. She wanted everyone to understand that harm to one part of the ecosystem damages all the other parts, including humans.

Born on a Pennsylvania farm in 1907, Rachel grew up surrounded by nature. With the support of her mother, Rachel became an avid writer, and by the age of 10, some of her writing had been published in children's magazines.

After graduating from Pennsylvania College for Women, Rachel studied oceanography and later earned a master's degree in zoology. Unfortunately, her dream of pursuing a PhD was dashed due to financial struggles during the **Great Depression**.

Rachel began her career as a writer for the US Bureau of Fisheries in 1936 and later was promoted to editor-in-chief of all publications for the US Fish and Wildlife Service. After relocating to Maryland, Rachel received a letter from a friend in Massachusetts who recounted an alarming number of birds dying after a pesticide was sprayed. After performing extensive research, Rachel wrote *Silent Spring*

DDT is a powerful pesticide that used to be popular among farmers seeking to protect their crops from insects. However, the spray soon began to upset the ecosystem because it is toxic to all animals, not just harmful insects. Rachel Carson discussed the dangers of DDT in her book, which led to its ban in 1972.

1950—IN JUNE, THE KOREAN WAR BEGINS.

1950—IN OCTOBER, THE COMIC STRIP *PEANUTS* IS FIRST PUBLISHED.

in 1962; the book focused on warning the public about the long-term effect of pesticides on ecosystems and humans, including cancer risks. Additionally, she called on public officials to investigate the chemicals being sprayed.

Chemical companies tried to cast doubt on Rachel's research; however, millions of citizens began to ask questions, and President John F. Kennedy commissioned an investigation into the pesticides. Rachel received medals and awards for her efforts in bringing the dangerous overuse of chemicals like DDT to the attention of the public.

After a battle with breast cancer, Rachel died in 1964, two years after *Silent Spring*'s publication. She was posthumously awarded the Presidential Medal of Freedom in 1980.

COMING UP: BOTH PIONEERS IN THEIR RESPECTIVE SPECIALTIES, RACHEL CARSON LAUNCHED THE ENVIRONMENTAL MOVEMENT WHILE VIRGINIA APGAR DEVELOPED A LIFE-SAVING EVALUATION FOR NEWBORN BABIES.

1951—THE FIRST LIVE TRANSCONTINENTAL TELEVISION BROADCAST OCCURS.

1953—DWIGHT D. EISENHOWER IS INAUGURATED AS THE 34TH PRESIDENT OF THE UNITED STATES.

VIRGINIA APGAR
(1909-1974)

INVENTOR OF THE APGAR SCORE

Restricted from becoming a surgeon, Virginia Apgar still managed to make major contributions to the fields of anesthesiology and **neonatal medicine**.

Born in 1909 in New Jersey, Virginia played the violin and showed an interest in science. Her love of science may have been inspired by her father, who kept a basement laboratory full of science experiments.

After earning her bachelor's degree in 1929, Virginia enrolled in the College of Physicians and Surgeons at Columbia University. Despite the widespread financial hardships of the Great Depression years, she graduated with a medical degree in 1933.

Although Virginia dreamed of becoming a surgeon, she found it nearly impossible to continue surgical training. Surgery was a specialty that seemed off-limits to women. So a mentor encouraged Virginia to work in the field of **anesthesia**.

DURING HER CAREER as a physician, Virginia Apgar noticed that the first few minutes of life are critical and should be used to evaluate the heart rate, breathing, muscle tone, color, and reflexes of newborn babies. Today, the Apgar Newborn Scoring System is used to monitor the health of newborns all over the world.

After some training, Virginia returned to Columbia University to build the anesthesia department. When demand for more anesthesia training increased, Virginia took on the responsibility of teaching other doctors how to practice this specialty and became the university's first female full professor.

An area of particular interest to Virginia was how anesthesia given to mothers during childbirth affected their babies. She developed and published the Apgar score in

1953—THE KOREAN WAR ENDS.

1954—IN JANUARY, THE TOURNAMENT OF ROSES PARADE IS THE FIRST EVENT NATIONALLY TELEVISED IN COLOR.

1949 to provide doctors with a quick, but comprehensive, method for evaluating a newborn's health in the minutes after birth.

Virginia continued her education at Johns Hopkins University, ultimately earning a master's degree in public health. Virginia made a lasting impact on the fields of anesthesiology and neonatal care through her groundbreaking research and her efforts to train doctors. Virginia died in 1974 at 65 years old.

COMING UP: WHILE VIRGINIA APGAR WAS DOING PIONEERING WORK IN THE FIELDS OF ANESTHESIOLOGY AND NEONATAL MEDICINE, ROSA PARKS WAS RESISTING UNFAIR TREATMENT.

1954–IN MAY, THE SUPREME COURT DECLARES RACIAL SEGREGATION IN PUBLIC SCHOOLS TO BE UNCONSTITUTIONAL IN *BROWN V. BOARD OF EDUCATION OF TOPEKA.*

1954–THE TERM "ROCK AND ROLL" IS COINED AND THE MUSIC BECOMES POPULAR.

ROSA PARKS
(1913-2005)
CIVIL RIGHTS ACTIVIST

Rosa Parks is best remembered for her refusal to give up her seat on a segregated city bus, but she was active in the civil rights movement long before December 1, 1955.

Born in 1913 in Alabama, Rosa grew up in a religious home and was raised primarily by her mother, a school teacher, after her parents separated. Rosa attended school and completed the 11th grade at the Alabama State Teachers College for Negroes. After marrying at 19 years old, Rosa earned her high school diploma.

Introduced to civil rights activism by her husband, Raymond Parks, Rosa joined the National Association for the Advancement of Colored People (NAACP) in 1943 and immediately became active in the organization.

In 1955, the **segregation** of schools had been ruled unconstitutional, but many other parts of society remained segregated, including the city buses of Montgomery, Alabama. On December 1, 1955, Rosa boarded the city bus after work and sat in the middle section of the bus, which was open to blacks or whites. Soon, the whites-only section of the bus was full. When the bus driver instructed Rosa to move to the back of the bus, she refused to leave her seat.

Rosa was arrested and fingerprinted, and spent a short time in jail. Soon after, African Americans in Montgomery, Alabama, participated in a bus boycott, capturing national attention and leading to the desegregation of city buses.

THE MONTGOMERY bus boycott was a peaceful 381-day boycott of city buses. For over a year, African Americans stayed off the buses, choosing instead to walk or carpool to get to work. The boycott led to a ruling that the segregation of buses was unconstitutional.

1955—THE VIETNAM WAR BEGINS.

1956—THE FIRST INTERSTATE HIGHWAY IS CONSTRUCTED AS PART OF THE FEDERAL AID HIGHWAY ACT.

Rosa and her husband faced tough consequences due to their involvement in the boycott, including the loss of Rosa's job and the refusal of employers to hire either spouse. After the boycott, Rosa and her husband settled in Detroit, Michigan, where they became active in Detroit's civil rights movement. Rosa died at 92 years old in 2005.

COMING UP: ROSA PARKS WAS WORKING TO PROMOTE THE CIVIL RIGHTS MOVEMENT AS MARGUERITE HIGGINS WAS REPORTING FROM THE FRONT LINES OF WORLD WAR II AND THE KOREAN WAR.

1957—THE SPACE RACE BETWEEN THE UNITED STATES AND THE SOVIET UNION BEGINS.

1958—NASA IS FOUNDED.

MARGUERITE HIGGINS
(1920-1966)
REPORTER AND WAR CORRESPONDENT

Journalist Marguerite Higgins refused to accept the lesser assignments usually given to women and worked her way into getting overseas assignments, becoming a world-renowned international reporter.

Marguerite, born in 1920, was the only child of an American World War I pilot and his French wife. Unable to find a job after earning a bachelor's degree, she worked toward a master's degree in journalism and graduated in 1942. After being hired to work full-time at the *New-York Tribune*, Marguerite was not satisfied with simple stories; she wanted top assignments covering events overseas.

Finally, in 1945, Marguerite was given an assignment in Germany. World War II was ending, but there were still important stories to report. She was one of a few reporters given access to parts of Germany destroyed by bombs, and she witnessed the freeing of Holocaust survivors from Nazi concentration camps. Once the war concluded, Marguerite continued to cover stories in Europe, like the Nuremberg trials, in which Nazi leaders were tried as war criminals.

IN APRIL 1945, Marguerite Higgins accompanied Allied soldiers to Dachau, a Nazi concentration camp. Jewish men, women, and children had been held at the camp in unimaginable conditions for years. Marguerite witnessed the liberation, or release, of prisoners from that camp and was the first American correspondent to write a report on the horrors of Dachau.

In 1950, Marguerite was reassigned to Japan. At first, she was unhappy about this move. But the next month, conflict broke out in the region. The Korean War began when communist North Korea invaded US-protected

1959—ALASKA AND HAWAII BECOME THE 49TH AND 50TH STATES ADMITTED TO THE UNION.

1960—THE FIRST TELEVISED US PRESIDENTIAL DEBATE IS HELD BETWEEN JOHN F. KENNEDY AND RICHARD NIXON.

South Korea. Marguerite immediately set to work, reporting on conditions in the capital of South Korea before the North Koreans took control of the city.

Now a well-respected journalist, Marguerite continued to report on stories like communist life in the Soviet Union, civil war in the Congo, and military action in Vietnam. She won multiple awards, like the Pulitzer Prize for International Reporting. Upon returning to Vietnam in 1965, Marguerite contracted a tropical disease, leishmaniasis, and had to be taken back to the United States. Sadly, she never recovered and died in 1966.

COMING UP: WHILE MARGUERITE HIGGINS DEVOTED HER LIFE TO REPORTING FROM THE FRONT LINES OF WAR, MARIA TALLCHIEF OVERCAME DISCRIMINATION TO BECOME THE FIRST NATIVE AMERICAN PRIMA BALLERINA.

1961—IN JANUARY, JOHN F. KENNEDY IS INAUGURATED AS THE 35TH PRESIDENT OF THE UNITED STATES.

1961—IN MAY, ALAN SHEPARD BECOMES THE FIRST AMERICAN IN SPACE.

MARIA TALLCHIEF
(1925-2013)
FIRST NATIVE AMERICAN PRIMA BALLERINA

orn Elizabeth "Betty" Marie Tall Chief, talented young dancer Maria Tallchief was turned away from multiple dance companies because of her Native American identity. Maria, determined to dance professionally, continued to pursue a dancing career and eventually became one of the most famous ballerinas in American history.

Born on the Osage reservation in Oklahoma in 1925, Maria excelled in dancing and playing music from an early age. After high school, Maria went to New York City to focus on ballet dancing. After much rejection and discrimination, Maria secured an understudy position in the

Ballet Russe de Monte Carlo, a Russian ballet company operating in the United States. Soon after, Maria was asked to replace a lead ballerina, thrilling critics with her incredible performance.

Maria continued her ballet career and soon attracted the attention

AFTER HER HIGH SCHOOL graduation, Betty Marie Tall Chief relocated to New York to work with the Ballet Russe de Monte Carlo. Upon being asked to change her name, she compromised and began to go by Maria Tallchief. A proud member of the Osage Nation, Maria refused to change her name to hide her heritage.

of George Balanchine, a famous **choreographer**. The couple married in 1946 and established the Ballet Society, today known as the New York City Ballet. She was both the first American and first Native American dancer to be named prima ballerina, the lead female dancer in a ballet company.

Upon retiring from her prima ballerina position in 1966, Maria continued to work in the dance world. She

1962–JOHN GLENN BECOMES THE FIRST AMERICAN ASTRONAUT IN ORBIT.

1963–MARTIN LUTHER KING, JR., DELIVERS HIS "I HAVE A DREAM" SPEECH ON THE STEPS OF THE LINCOLN MEMORIAL.

served as an artistic director for the Lyric Opera of Chicago and later founded the Chicago City Ballet.

Maria received many honors throughout her lifetime, including the National Medal of the Arts. Her native state, Oklahoma, honored her by declaring June 29, 1953, Maria Tallchief Day. Maria and four other Native American, Oklahoma-born prima ballerinas were featured in a mural, *Flight of Spirit*, that hangs in the Oklahoma State Capitol.

COMING UP: MARIA TALLCHIEF ROSE TO FAME IN THE WORLD OF BALLET, WHILE CORETTA SCOTT KING WAS FIGHTING FOR CIVIL RIGHTS ALONGSIDE HER HUSBAND, MARTIN LUTHER KING, JR.

1963—IN NOVEMBER, PRESIDENT JOHN F. KENNEDY IS ASSASSINATED; VICE PRESIDENT LYNDON B. JOHNSON BECOMES THE 36TH PRESIDENT OF THE UNITED STATES.

1965—IN FEBRUARY, MALCOM X IS ASSASSINATED IN HARLEM, NEW YORK.

CORETTA SCOTT KING
(1927-2006)
CIVIL RIGHTS LEADER

Coretta Scott King crafted a meaningful legacy of leadership and peaceful protests. She worked on behalf of those who were living in poverty and individuals facing discrimination, among others.

Born in 1927 in Alabama, Coretta was a talented singer and played several instruments; later she earned a bachelor's degree in music. While attending the New England Conservatory of Music in Boston, Coretta was introduced to Martin Luther King, Jr., a doctoral student. The couple married in 1953.

After graduation, Coretta and Martin relocated to Alabama, where Martin had been named pastor of Dexter Avenue Baptist Church. This church became heavily involved in the civil rights movement, leading to vandalism as well as death threats for the pastor and his family. Coretta was often seen by her husband's side, helping fight for justice. As the movement spread to more cities, Coretta traveled with her husband to teach his philosophy of nonviolent civil disobedience.

Coretta had many accomplishments of her own. Using her background in music, Coretta designed and performed in "freedom concerts" to tell the story of the civil rights movement through song, poetry, and

IN AUGUST 1963, around 250,000 people gathered in Washington, DC, near the Lincoln Memorial to protest the unfair treatment continually faced by African Americans. This massive protest was named the March on Washington for Jobs and Freedom and became the site of Martin Luther King, Jr.'s influential "I Have a Dream" speech.

1965—THE UNITED STATES OFFICIALLY ENTERS THE VIETNAM WAR.

1967—THE FIRST SUPER BOWL IS PLAYED.

storytelling. She was the first woman to deliver the Class Day address at Harvard, the first woman to preach at St. Paul's Cathedral in London at a statutory service, and she served as a delegate to the Women's Strike for Peace in Switzerland.

After the **assassination** of her husband in 1968, Coretta continued to campaign against injustice. She marched in labor strikes, lectured about women's rights, racism, and economic issues, and later established the Martin Luther King, Jr., Center for Nonviolent Social Change. Coretta died on January 30, 2006, and is buried next to her husband in Atlanta.

COMING UP: WHILE CORETTA SCOTT KING WAS PROMOTING PEACEFUL SOCIAL CHANGE, MURIEL SIEBERT WAS FEARLESSLY INFILTRATING WALL STREET, BECOMING THE FIRST FEMALE MEMBER OF THE NEW YORK STOCK EXCHANGE.

1968–IN APRIL, MARTIN LUTHER KING, JR., IS ASSASSINATED IN MEMPHIS, TENNESSEE.

1968–IN JUNE, SHIRLEY CHISHOLM BECOMES THE FIRST AFRICAN AMERICAN WOMAN ELECTED TO CONGRESS.

MURIEL SIEBERT

(1928–2013)

FIRST WOMAN TO OWN A SEAT ON THE NEW YORK STOCK EXCHANGE

Called the "First Woman of Finance," Muriel Siebert worked her way up on Wall Street, from research trainee to seat owner on the New York Stock Exchange (NYSE), and opened the door for women to work in the world of finance.

Muriel, born in 1928, dreamed of working at the NYSE. She enrolled in Western Reserve University and attended business classes until she was forced to leave school early due to her father's cancer diagnosis.

Around 1954, Muriel moved to New York City to seek employment on Wall Street, home of the NYSE. Refusing to settle for a job as a secretary, Muriel lied and told prospective employers that she had a college degree and eventually landed a job as a research trainee.

BUYING A SEAT on the New York Stock Exchange (NYSE) was not as simple as being able to afford it. Prospective owners had to go through a thorough review process and were held to high ethical standards once accepted. Buying a seat on the NYSE is no longer possible because in 2006, the exchange became a public company.

Refusing to do the same work as men for less pay, Muriel moved through various brokerage firms.

Muriel made history in 1967 when she became the first woman to buy a seat on the New York Stock Exchange. Soon after, she established a firm, Muriel Siebert & Company.

For a decade she worked as the only female member of the stock exchange. However, in 1977, she temporarily

1969—IN JANUARY, RICHARD NIXON IS INAUGURATED AS THE 37TH PRESIDENT OF THE UNITED STATES.

1969—IN JULY, ASTRONAUT NEIL ARMSTRONG BECOMES THE FIRST MAN TO SET FOOT ON THE MOON.

left her firm to serve as the superintendent of banking for the state of New York, the first woman to ever hold that position. Overseeing all financial institutions in the state, Muriel ensured that not a single bank failed on her watch.

After a failed Senate campaign, Muriel returned to the NYSE and continued her financial work. Muriel is credited with creating a program to share her firm's profits with charities and developing a personal finance program to teach young people financial management skills. She died in 2013.

COMING UP: WHILE MURIEL SIEBERT FLOURISHED IN THE MALE-DOMINATED FINANCIAL SECTOR, MAYA ANGELOU OVERCAME TRAUMA TO BECOME AN AUTHOR, SINGER, CIVIL RIGHTS ACTIVIST, POET, AND SCHOLAR.

1970—EARTH DAY IS OBSERVED FOR THE FIRST TIME.

1971—18-YEAR-OLDS GAIN THE RIGHT TO VOTE UNDER THE TWENTY-SIXTH AMENDMENT.

MAYA ANGELOU
(1928-2014)
WRITER; CIVIL RIGHTS ACTIVIST

Despite tragedy in her early years, Maya Angelou blossomed into a world-renowned author, singer, dancer, activist, and scholar.

Born in 1928 to unstable parents, Maya went to live with her grandmother in Arkansas as a young child. Her early life was filled with anguish and heartache. After a traumatic incident that occurred during a visit to her mother's home in St. Louis, Maya did not speak for nearly six years.

While attending high school in California, she became the first African American female streetcar conductor in the city of San Francisco. As a young adult, Maya studied drama and dance and performed in multiple successful productions around the world. When she lived in New York City, Maya became involved

AFRICAN AMERICAN authors founded the Harlem Writers Guild in New York City in 1950 because they felt that African American literature was underappreciated by white critics. The guild helped launch the careers of many prominent authors, and it is still in existence today.

in the civil rights movement and joined the Harlem Writers Guild, an organization dedicated to helping black authors.

For part of the 1960s, Maya lived and worked in Egypt and Ghana as a writer and university administrator. Maya published the first part of her autobiography, *I Know Why the Caged Bird Sings,* in 1970. During the following decades, she wrote and published the remaining sections of her autobiography along with many other books of essays and poetry.

1972—IN FEBRUARY, RICHARD NIXON BECOMES THE FIRST SITTING PRESIDENT OF THE UNITED STATES TO SET FOOT INTO THE PEOPLE'S REPUBLIC OF CHINA.

1972—IN SEPTEMBER, THE FIRST COMMERCIAL HOME VIDEO GAME CONSOLE IS CREATED.

For the rest of her life, Maya fully immersed herself in writing, directing, acting, and producing. In 1972, she became the first African American woman to have her screenplay made into a film. She was awarded many honorary degrees. She died in 2014 at 86 years old.

COMING UP: WHILE MAYA ANGELOU WAS INSPIRING MANY WITH HER MULTIFACETED CAREER, DOLORES HUERTA WAS WORKING TO IMPROVE THE LIVES AND WORKING CONDITIONS OF FARMWORKERS.

1973—*SKYLAB* IS LAUNCHED, BECOMING THE UNITED STATES' FIRST SPACE STATION.

1974—PRESIDENT RICHARD NIXON BECOMES THE FIRST PRESIDENT TO RESIGN FROM OFFICE.

DOLORES HUERTA

(1930-)

LABOR LEADER; COFOUNDER OF THE NATIONAL FARM WORKERS ASSOCIATION

Frustrated by the poor treatment of farmworkers, Dolores Huerta devoted her life to improving pay, safety, and work conditions for the men, women, and children who performed **agricultural** work.

Dolores was born in New Mexico in 1930 to Alicia and Juan Fernandez. Her father was a farmworker and later a state legislator. After her parents divorced, Dolores moved to Stockton, California, with her mother and siblings. While her mother worked two jobs, Dolores attended school and noticed the discrimination directed at her and other Latina and Latino children.

Dolores, determined not to let discrimination stop her, graduated from high school and enrolled in college. She earned a degree and teaching license but only worked as a teacher for a short time because she thought she could do more to help her students as an organizer. After Dolores left the classroom, she worked with the Stockton Community Service Organization, organizing voter registration drives and pushing for community improvements.

Following the community-minded, compassionate example of her mother, Dolores helped cofound the National Farm Workers Association in 1962 with

DURING THE 1970S, Dolores Huerta coordinated nationwide boycotts of agricultural products like grapes, lettuce, and wine. The political climate created by these boycotts led lawmakers in California to establish the Agricultural Labor Relations Board in 1975. The purpose of the board is to help resolve disputes and get justice for agricultural workers.

1975—THE VIETNAM WAR ENDS.

1976—APPLE COMPUTER IS FOUNDED.

the help of fellow activist César Chávez. Their organization was later renamed the United Farm Workers of America (UFW). Dolores negotiated with lawmakers to help farmworkers receive government benefits and disability insurance. She also advocated for safer working conditions and the banning of harmful chemicals and pesticides.

Continuing her involvement with UFW, Dolores became involved in politics and helped elect candidates who supported the rights of farmworkers. Additionally, she served on the US Commission on Agricultural Workers from 1988 to 1993.

Dolores has received numerous awards and honorary doctoral degrees, including the Presidential Medal of Freedom in 2012.

COMING UP: ALTHOUGH THEY SERVED IN VASTLY DIFFERENT CIRCUMSTANCES, BOTH DOLORES HUERTA AND SANDRA DAY O'CONNOR DEDICATED THEIR LIVES TO SERVING OTHERS.

1979—AMERICAN AIRLINES FLIGHT 191 CRASHES, BECOMING THE WORST AVIATION ACCIDENT IN US HISTORY.

1981—RONALD REAGAN IS INAUGURATED AS THE 40TH PRESIDENT OF THE UNITED STATES.

SANDRA DAY O'CONNOR

(1930-)

FIRST FEMALE JUSTICE ON THE SUPREME COURT

Defying the gender discrimination that plagued the law profession in the 1950s, Sandra Day O'Connor proved her devotion to justice. She worked in a variety of legal positions and later was appointed to the Supreme Court, the highest court in the United States.

Sandra was born in 1930 in El Paso, Texas, and spent much of her childhood on her family's ranch in Arizona. After graduating from high school, Sandra attended Stanford University, where she earned a bachelor's degree and a law degree.

Despite having the same law degree as her male peers, Sandra was repeatedly turned away from jobs because she was a woman. However, she was able to gain a position in 1952 as a deputy district attorney in California, and soon after, she served in Germany as a civil attorney for the US Army.

When Sandra returned to the United States, she worked as a private practice lawyer and became involved in politics. She served in a variety of public positions, including as an assistant attorney general and as a judge for the Arizona Court of Appeals. Her highest appointment occurred in 1981 when President Ronald Reagan chose Sandra as his nominee for the Supreme Court. She was unanimously confirmed to the position by the Senate. Sandra made history as the first female associate justice on the Supreme Court.

WHEN SUPREME COURT Justice Sandra Day O'Connor retired from the bench, she continued her public service by creating iCivics. The mission of this website is to increase students' knowledge of civics, or the study of the rights and duties of citizenship. Students investigate and argue real cases to help them learn about the US court system.

1981—MTV IS LAUNCHED.

1983—ASTRONAUT SALLY RIDE BECOMES THE FIRST AMERICAN WOMAN IN SPACE.

As an associate justice, Sandra was admired for her practical approach to decisions and her loyalty to the US Constitution. She issued numerous opinions throughout her time on the court upholding religious liberty and freedom of speech and guarding against gender discrimination.

Due to health concerns, Sandra retired from the court in 2006 after serving for 24 years. To honor her service, President Barack Obama awarded Sandra the Presidential Medal of Freedom in 2009.

COMING UP: BOTH SANDRA DAY O'CONNOR AND GLORIA STEINEM WERE TRAILBLAZERS WHO HELPED OPEN OPPORTUNITIES FOR WOMEN.

1984—THE FIRST HANDHELD CELL PHONE IS SOLD.

1986—THE *CHALLENGER* SPACE SHUTTLE EXPLODES AFTER TAKEOFF IN CAPE CANAVERAL, FLORIDA, KILLING ALL SEVEN CREWMEMBERS ABOARD.

GLORIA STEINEM
(1934-)

FEMINIST LEADER; COFOUNDER OF *MS.* MAGAZINE

Gloria Steinem survived a difficult childhood and rose above gender discrimination to become a celebrated journalist and spokeswoman of the women's rights movement.

Born in 1934 in Ohio, Gloria spent her early years moving from town to town in a house trailer with her mother and father, a traveling salesman. When her parents divorced, Gloria settled with her mother in Toledo, Ohio, and was finally able to attend school regularly.

After graduating from Smith College in 1956, Gloria studied in India and was introduced to activism when she took part in nonviolent protests there. Upon moving to New York City in 1960, Gloria began working as a journalist and was frustrated with the lifestyle and fashion articles she was asked to write. She wanted to write about more serious topics like politics.

After working hard to establish herself in the journalistic community, Gloria became a founding columnist at *New York* magazine. Finally able to report on political and social issues, Gloria became an outspoken proponent of the women's rights movement, particularly with respect to women's health and **autonomy** over their own bodies.

THE TAKE OUR DAUGHTERS to Work Day project, launched during the 1990s, was created by Gloria Steinem and the Ms. Foundation for Women to let girls see real-life female role models working in different professions. In 2003, the program expanded to include boys and is now called Take Our Daughters and Sons to Work Day.

1989—THE ANIMATED COMEDY *THE SIMPSONS* DEBUTS ON TELEVISION.

1990—THE HUBBLE SPACE TELESCOPE IS LAUNCHED.

In 1971, Gloria partnered with other female journalists to found *Ms.* magazine in an effort to further the discussion about women's rights.

Gloria has spent many years participating in women's rights causes. She founded or helped found organizations including the Women's Media Center, dedicated to furthering the voices of women in media, and the Ms. Foundation for Women. In 2013, she received the Presidential Medal of Freedom.

COMING UP: WHILE GLORIA STEINEM INSPIRED WOMEN WITH HER JOURNALISTIC TALENTS AND PASSION FOR WOMEN'S RIGHTS, BARBARA JORDAN TACKLED SOCIAL ISSUES AND CIVIL RIGHTS THROUGH HER WORK IN LAW AND POLITICS.

1990–THE GULF WAR BEGINS.

1991–THE GULF WAR ENDS.

BARBARA JORDAN
(1936-1996)

CONGRESSWOMAN; CIVIL RIGHTS LEADER

A fierce supporter of the US Constitution, Barbara Jordan advocated for civil rights and racial equality.

Barbara was born in 1936 and raised in an impoverished area of Houston where she attended racially segregated schools. In high school and college, she made a name for herself as a gifted public speaker and debate team member.

After her law school graduation, Barbara opened her own law office from her parents' home in Texas. Barbara soon became involved in politics by campaigning for others and later running for office herself. Although she lost the first two elections, Barbara was determined not to give up. She was elected to the Texas Senate in 1966.

Although she faced gender and racial discrimination in the Texas Senate, Barbara pressed on and authored the first Texas state law on the

IN 1974, Barbara Jordan made a passionate speech supporting the Constitution. She reminded members of Congress that African Americans were not always included in government processes when she said, "But through the process of amendment, interpretation, and court decision, I have finally been included in 'We, the People.'"

minimum wage. Later, in 1972, Barbara was elected to the US House of Representatives, where she worked on legislation that strengthened civil rights, voting rights, and programs for minorities and the poor.

Barbara is perhaps best known for her participation in the hearings of the House Judiciary Committee concerning the **impeachment** of President Richard Nixon. Broadcasted nationwide, Barbara soon became known for

1991—IN AUGUST, THE WORLD WIDE WEB IS PUBLICLY LAUNCHED.

1991—IN DECEMBER, THE COLD WAR ENDS AS THE SOVIET UNION IS DISSOLVED.

her intense questioning of witnesses and promotion of the US Constitution.

Serious health issues forced Barbara to resign from politics in 1979. However, she continued to share her knowledge and experience as a professor and ethics advisor at the Lyndon B. Johnson School of Public Affairs. To honor her contributions to the United States, President Bill Clinton awarded her the Presidential Medal of Freedom in 1994. Sadly, Barbara died in Texas in 1996. She was the first African American buried in the Texas State Cemetery.

COMING UP: BARBARA JORDAN WAS MAKING A DIFFERENCE IN US GOVERNMENT AS MARIAN WRIGHT EDELMAN WAS HELPING IMPROVE THE LIVES OF CHILDREN.

1992—VIOLENCE BREAKS OUT IN LOS ANGELES AFTER FOUR POLICEMEN ARE ACQUITTED OF THE BEATING OF RODNEY KING.

1993—BILL CLINTON IS INAUGURATED AS THE 42ND PRESIDENT OF THE UNITED STATES.

MARIAN WRIGHT EDELMAN
(1939-)
ACTIVIST FOR CHILDREN'S RIGHTS

Committed to making a difference in the lives of children, Marian Wright Edelman founded the Children's Defense Fund (CDF).

Marian was born in South Carolina in 1939 to a Baptist minister and his wife. She learned from her parents that faith required public service. Although Marian was forced to attend racially segregated schools with fewer opportunities available than at white schools, she was an excellent student. She graduated from high school, attended

Spelman College, and earned scholarships that allowed her to study in Switzerland, France, and the Soviet Union.

THE MISSION of the CDF is to give every child a healthy start and violence-free communities and to end child poverty. The CDF gives special attention to foster children and children involved in the juvenile justice system.

A young woman when the civil rights movement began to spread, Marian decided that she would contribute by studying law. She enrolled at Yale Law School and graduated in 1963. Marian soon went to work for the National Association for the Advancement of Colored People (NAACP) Legal Defense and Educational Fund. Upon relocating to Mississippi to continue her work with the NAACP, Marian made history as the first African American woman accepted into the Mississippi state bar.

In 1964, Marian began work as a lawyer for the Child Development Group in Mississippi and realized that she

1998–IN SEPTEMBER, GOOGLE, INC. IS FOUNDED.

1998–IN NOVEMBER, THE *INTERNATIONAL SPACE STATION* IS LAUNCHED.

enjoyed helping children. Marian married Peter Edelman, a lawyer and policymaker, in 1968 and the couple relocated to Washington, DC. Moving to the nation's capital allowed Marian to talk with lawmakers about her vision to help people living in poverty, especially children.

In 1973, Marian founded the CDF. The CDF quickly became a successful organization with the mission of advocating for children, including preventing child abuse and drug abuse, while encouraging healthy habits and education.

To honor her writing and humanitarian efforts, Marian has received multiple awards, including the Robert F. Kennedy Lifetime Achievement Award.

COMING UP: WHILE MARIAN WRIGHT EDELMAN WORKED TO IMPROVE THE LIVES OF CHILDREN, BILLIE JEAN KING, A PROFESSIONAL TENNIS PLAYER, ADVOCATED FOR THE RIGHTS OF FEMALE ATHLETES.

1999—PRESIDENT BILL CLINTON IS THE SECOND PRESIDENT OF THE UNITED STATES TO BE IMPEACHED.

2000—THE FEARED Y2K CRISIS FAILS TO MATERIALIZE.

BILLIE JEAN KING

(1943-)

PROFESSIONAL TENNIS PLAYER WHO ADVOCATED FOR THE RIGHTS OF FEMALE PLAYERS

Frustrated by the lack of equality in professional tennis, Billie Jean King pushed for the equal treatment of women in sports.

Billie was born in 1943 in California to a firefighter and his wife. Billie's family was athletically inclined, and both Billie and her brother, Randy, grew up to be professional athletes.

When introduced to tennis around age 11, Billie knew instantly that it would be her favorite sport. Once she had earned the money, Billie purchased her first tennis racket and began to play on her city's public courts. At age 14, Billie won her first tennis championship.

IN 1973, Bobby Riggs, claiming that men had superior tennis skills, challenged Billie Jean King to a match. The highly televised match was called the "Battle of the Sexes" because a female player was competing against a male player. Billie won the match and received a large cash prize.

In 1961, Billie competed in England in her first Wimbledon tournament. Billie and her tennis partner, Karen Hantze, became the youngest two-person team to win the Wimbledon women's doubles title. In 1966, Billie was named number one in the world in women's tennis. She went on to win numerous titles in the United States, England, France, and Australia.

When Billie Jean King won the US Open tennis tournament in 1972, she was awarded a large amount of money, but it was $15,000 less than the men's champion received. This injustice motivated Billie to begin advocating for equal prize money for both male and female champions.

2001—IN JANUARY, GEORGE W. BUSH IS INAUGURATED AS THE 43RD PRESIDENT OF THE UNITED STATES.

2001—ON SEPTEMBER 11, THE WORLD TRADE CENTER AND PENTAGON ARE ATTACKED BY FOREIGN TERRORISTS. THE WAR ON TERROR BEGINS.

In 1984, Billie announced her retirement from competitive tennis. However, she remained active in coaching and continued to advocate for equal rights. Billie was the first woman to have a major sports venue named after her. In 2006, the National Tennis Center, where the US Open is played, was renamed the Billie Jean King National Tennis Center. In 2009, she received the Presidential Medal of Freedom, honoring her work to promote equality for women and for lesbian, gay, bisexual, transgender, queer, asexual, and gender non-conforming individuals, among many more (LGBTQ+). She lives in New York with her partner, also a former professional tennis player.

COMING UP: AS BILLIE JEAN KING'S PROFESSIONAL TENNIS CAREER WAS WINDING DOWN, SALLY RIDE SOARED INTO SPACE AND ON EARTH SOUGHT TO IMPROVE SCIENCE EDUCATION.

2001—IN OCTOBER, THE UNITED STATES INVADES AFGHANISTAN, IGNITING THE WAR IN AFGHANISTAN.

2003—THE IRAQ WAR BEGINS.

SALLY RIDE
(1951–2012)

FIRST FEMALE AMERICAN ASTRONAUT IN SPACE

Paving the way for future female astronauts, Sally Ride became the first American woman to enter space.

Sally was born in 1951 in California. Encouraged to pursue her interests by her parents, Sally became an award-winning tennis player. She attended Stanford University, earning two bachelor's degrees, a master of science degree, and a doctoral degree in physics.

In 1977, Sally saw a newspaper ad that changed the course of her future. The National Aeronautics and Space Administration (NASA) was searching for young scientists to train as astronauts, and women were welcome to apply.

Sally sent in her application and was chosen as one of six female astronaut candidates in January 1978.

Sally's astronaut training included experiencing weightlessness, water survival, and parachute jumping, but Sally especially loved flight training. Chosen to be a mission specialist aboard the shuttle *Challenger*, Sally made history in 1983 as the first American woman in space.

During the week-long mission, Sally was the flight engineer. Her duties included launching communication satellites and operating the shuttle's robotic arm. Soon, Sally was in space again. Her second flight launched in October 1984, making her the first American woman to fly into space a second time.

ON JANUARY 29, 1986, the *Challenger* shuttle was scheduled to take off from Cape Canaveral, Florida. The seven-member crew, including school teacher Christa McAuliffe, boarded the spacecraft to prepare for takeoff. Seventy-three seconds after launch, tragedy struck when the shuttle broke apart, ultimately killing all on board.

2003–IN FEBRUARY, THE SPACE SHUTTLE *COLUMBIA* DISASTER OCCURS.

2003–IN AUGUST, THE SOCIAL NETWORKING WEBSITE MYSPACE IS LAUNCHED.

Sally was assigned to a third space mission, but crew training immediately stopped due to the *Challenger* disaster in 1986. Upon retirement from NASA in 1987, she continued to work in the field of science. Believing in the importance of science education for students, especially girls, Sally wrote science books for children.

Sadly, Sally struggled with pancreatic cancer and died in 2012 at the age of 61. In 2013, Sally was posthumously awarded the Presidential Medal of Freedom.

COMING UP: WHILE SALLY RIDE WAS MAKING HISTORY AS THE FIRST AMERICAN WOMAN IN SPACE, OPRAH WINFREY WAS BREAKING RECORDS AS A TALK SHOW HOST, PRODUCER, ACTRESS, AND PHILANTHROPIST.

2004–FACEBOOK IS LAUNCHED.

2005–HURRICANE KATRINA DEVASTATES THE SOUTHEASTERN UNITED STATES, FLOODING THE CITY OF NEW ORLEANS IN THE COSTLIEST NATURAL DISASTER IN US HISTORY.

OPRAH WINFREY

(1954-)

MEDIA EXECUTIVE AND PHILANTHROPIST

Despite a challenging early childhood, Oprah Winfrey became one of the most successful women in the history of the United States.

Born into poverty in 1954, Oprah lacked a stable home life. She was raised by her grandmother on a rural farm until age six. Then she went to live with her mother in a poor, dangerous area in Wisconsin, where she was abused. However, when Oprah was sent to Tennessee to live with her father as a teenager, she began to feel more secure. Her father provided structure and rules, requiring weekly book reports and new vocabulary words daily.

Years later, Oprah said, "When my father took me, it changed the course of my life. He saved me."

In high school, Oprah was an excellent student and worked with a local radio station to deliver afternoon newscasts. By the time she was a sophomore in college, Oprah was Nashville's first African American female news anchor.

OPRAH is one of the wealthiest self-made women in the United States and is admired for her philanthropic, or charitable, work. She has given away hundreds of millions of dollars across a range of causes including opening a school for girls in South Africa, providing scholarships to 400 attendees of Morehouse College in Atlanta, and helping people rebuild their homes after Hurricane Katrina.

After her college graduation, Oprah worked at various news stations and later hosted her own talk show. *AM Chicago* went from last to first in ratings within months and was renamed *The Oprah Winfrey Show*, which became one of the most successful television shows in history.

2006—TWITTER IS LAUNCHED.

2007—NANCY PELOSI BECOMES THE FIRST FEMALE SPEAKER OF THE HOUSE OF REPRESENTATIVES.

Oprah's next challenge was acting, and although she had little experience, she was chosen to appear in *The Color Purple*. She formed her own television production company, Harpo Productions, Inc., in 1986 and later launched a film production company and her own cable channel.

COMING UP: WHILE OPRAH WINFREY WAS BREAKING RECORDS IN THE MEDIA INDUSTRY, SONIA SOTOMAYOR WAS SERVING AS A LAWYER, AND EVENTUALLY BECAME A SUPREME COURT JUSTICE.

2007–IN DECEMBER, THE GREAT RECESSION IN THE UNITED STATES BEGINS FOLLOWING THE COLLAPSE OF THE US REAL ESTATE MARKET AND HOUSING BUBBLE.

2008–NASA'S *PHOENIX* SPACECRAFT BECOMES THE FIRST TO LAND ON THE NORTHERN POLAR REGION OF MARS.

SONIA SOTOMAYOR
(1954-)

FIRST LATINA SUPREME COURT JUSTICE

Sonia Sotomayor rose from humble conditions to become a lawyer, judge, and the first Latina individual to serve on the Supreme Court.

Born in 1954 in New York to parents who had immigrated from Puerto Rico, Sonia lost her father at the age of nine. While her mother worked long hours to support the family, Sonia committed herself to schoolwork and dreamed of becoming a lawyer one day.

After earning a bachelor's degree from Princeton University and a law degree from Yale Law School, Sonia served as an assistant district attorney in New York from 1979 to 1984. Later she worked at a private law firm, helping clients with copyright and intellectual property disputes.

In 1991, Sonia assumed the role of federal judge when she was appointed to the US District Court, Southern District of New

IN 1995, Major League Baseball was in trouble. Players were on strike and team owners were not budging. Sonia, then a federal judge, sided with the players because she thought that the teams' owners violated labor laws. Her decision forced both sides to resume negotiations, which allowed baseball games to resume. Sonia became known as "the woman who saved baseball."

York, by President George H. W. Bush. In 1998, Sonia was appointed by President Bill Clinton to serve as a judge on the US Court of Appeals for the Second Circuit, where Sonia acquired a reputation for delivering carefully researched decisions. While serving on the bench, Sonia

2009—BARACK OBAMA IS INAUGURATED AS THE 44TH PRESIDENT OF THE UNITED STATES, BECOMING THE FIRST AFRICAN AMERICAN US PRESIDENT IN HISTORY.

2009—THE GREAT RECESSION IN THE UNITED STATES OFFICIALLY ENDS.

taught aspiring lawyers at Columbia Law School and the New York University School of Law.

President Barack Obama nominated Sonia to the Supreme Court in 2009. The US Senate confirmed Sonia to the court, making her the first Latina Supreme Court justice and the third woman to be appointed to the court.

COMING UP: SONIA SOTOMAYOR'S CONTRIBUTIONS TO THE UNITED STATES INCLUDE HER WORK AS A LAWYER, JUDGE, AND SUPREME COURT JUSTICE; MEANWHILE MAYA LIN IS NATIONALLY RECOGNIZED FOR HER DESIGN OF THE VIETNAM VETERANS MEMORIAL IN WASHINGTON, DC.

2010—THE PATIENT PROTECTION AND AFFORDABLE CARE ACT, ALSO KNOWN AS OBAMACARE, IS SIGNED INTO LAW.

2010—IN APRIL, THE DEEPWATER HORIZON OIL RIG EXPLODES, THE WORST OIL SPILL IN US HISTORY.

MAYA LIN

(1959-)

ARCHITECT AND SCULPTOR; DESIGNER OF THE
VIETNAM VETERANS MEMORIAL

The talented Maya Lin shared her passion for architecture with Americans through her design for the Vietnam Veterans Memorial in Washington, DC.

Born in Ohio in 1959 to parents who had immigrated from China, Maya grew up helping in her father's ceramics studio. Maya excelled in school. She took college classes as a high school student and hoped to become an architect.

After high school, Maya enrolled in Yale University to study architecture. During her senior year of college,

Maya completed a class project in which she was asked to design a memorial to honor veterans of the Vietnam War. The Vietnam Veterans Memorial Fund hosted a national competition during which a design for the permanent memorial would be chosen.

WHEN MAYA'S DESIGN for the Vietnam Veterans Memorial was selected, the nation's involvement in the war was still highly controversial. Likewise, her design for the memorial sparked significant conflict. Ultimately, a compromise was reached and the memorial was built. Once it opened, the memorial's emotional power won the admiration of most of its former critics.

Twenty-one-year-old Maya submitted her design for consideration, and out of 1,421 entries, including her professor's, Maya's design was selected.

Maya's monument design honored the men and women who had served and perished in the Vietnam War. The monument contained two polished black granite walls inscribed with the names of the over 58,000 men and women killed or missing in Vietnam.

2010–IN OCTOBER, INSTAGRAM IS LAUNCHED.

2011–THE SPACE SHUTTLE PROGRAM ENDS AFTER 30 YEARS IN SERVICE.

Later, Maya was asked to design a monument to honor the civil rights movement in Alabama. The Civil Rights Memorial was dedicated in 1989.

Maya expanded from the creation of memorials to other types of architecture, including a pedestrian bridge and topiary park, and to sculptures and art installations. As an environmentalist her work is often inspired by the natural world. In 2016, Maya was awarded the Presidential Medal of Freedom.

COMING UP: MAYA LIN HAS SPARKED EMOTION AND THOUGHT WITH HER CREATIVE DESIGNS, WHILE MARY BONAUTO HAS SPARKED CHANGE ADVOCATING FOR THE RIGHTS OF SAME-SEX COUPLES.

2015—THE SUPREME COURT RULES IN *OBERGEFELL V. HODGES* THAT THE CONSTITUTION GUARANTEES THE RIGHT TO MARRY FOR SAME-SEX COUPLES.

2016—HILLARY RODHAM CLINTON BECOMES THE FIRST WOMAN NOMINATED FOR THE PRESIDENCY OF THE UNITED STATES BY A MAJOR POLITICAL PARTY.

MARY BONAUTO

(1961-)

CIVIL RIGHTS ADVOCATE FOR MARRIAGE EQUALITY

During her career as a lawyer, Mary Bonauto has fought against the discrimination that LGBTQ+ people often face in employment, housing, and other areas. Dedicating her life to advocating for civil rights for the LGBTQ+ community, Mary has helped spark numerous policy changes in the United States.

Born in 1961 to a strict Catholic family in New York, Mary worked hard in school, later graduating from the Northeastern University School of Law. She experienced discrimination when she came out in college, which she later said inspired her to help make things better for others. Upon joining a small law firm in Maine in 1987, Mary became one of only three openly gay lawyers practicing in the state.

To help LGBTQ+ people who face multiple forms of discrimination, Mary began work at the GLBTQ Legal Advocates & Defenders (GLAD) organization. She was involved in educational efforts and lawsuits in several New England states. In 1999, Mary argued in the case of *Baker v. Vermont*, challenging the denial of marriage to same-sex couples. Mary and her co-counsel were victorious in this case because the Vermont Supreme Court ruled that same-sex couples must be given the same protection and benefits as heterosexual couples. This ruling

IN 2015, Mary Bonauto argued before the Supreme Court on behalf of James Obergefell and other individuals to challenge bans on marriage between same-sex couples in Ohio, Michigan, Kentucky, and Tennessee. The Supreme Court ruled that states must allow marriage licenses for same-sex couples and also must recognize the marriages of same-sex couples from other states.

2017—ON JANUARY 20, DONALD J. TRUMP IS INAUGURATED AS THE 45TH PRESIDENT OF THE UNITED STATES.

2017—ON JANUARY 21, THE WOMEN'S MARCH BECOMES THE LARGEST SINGLE-DAY PROTEST IN US HISTORY.

was celebrated as America's first civil union law. But some states did not recognize civil unions made in other states. There was more work to do.

Later, Mary argued in the case of *Goodridge v. Department of Public Health* in Massachusetts. This case prompted Massachusetts to become the first state to allow legal marriages to same-sex couples in 2004. Mary continued her mission to help same-sex couples gain the right to marry by representing other cases.

Mary worked in federal court on behalf of same-sex couples, and eventually she stood before the Supreme Court, where in 2015 she challenged bans on same-sex couples' right to marriage. Her success led to legal marriage equality nationwide.

Mary was named "the country's most powerful lawyer in the marriage equality fight" by *The Advocate*. She has received numerous other titles and honors for her contributions to the LGBTQ+ community.

2019–IN APRIL, THE FIRST IMAGE OF A BLACK HOLE IS TAKEN.

2019–IN JUNE, DONALD J. TRUMP BECOMES THE FIRST SITTING PRESIDENT OF THE UNITED STATES TO SET FOOT IN NORTH KOREA.

GLOSSARY

Abolitionist: a person who wanted slavery to end

Activist: a person who advocates for a particular cause

Agricultural: having to do with the production of crops

Almshouses: housing, not always good, provided to the poor until the early 20th century

Ambassador: an authorized messenger or representative

Anesthesia: the administration of gases or drugs during surgical operations to reduce pain

Assassination: the killing of a politically prominent individual

Autonomy: personal decision-making power

Aviation: the use of aircraft, such as planes

Cholera: an infectious disease that causes severe vomiting and diarrhea

Choreographer: a person who arranges dance movements

Civilian: a person who is not involved in the military

Civil rights: full legal, economic, and social rights

Constellations: groupings of stars

Coup: a sudden, violent seizure of power from a government

Discrimination: the act of unfairly treating a person or group based on assigning them to a category, such as race or sex

Disenfranchisement: the state of being deprived of the right to vote

Domestic: relating to the home

Emancipated: set free

Epidemic: a disease that affects many people at the same time

Feminist: an advocate for the rights of women

Great Depression: a period of economic crisis that began with the stock market crash in 1929

Impeachment: the act of bringing formal charges against a public official

Indentured servant: a person who was required by contract to work for a specified period of time, often years, without direct wages, often as a means to settle debts or to obtain passage to the New World

Inferior: less important, valuable, or worthy

Infirmary: a place to care for sick or injured people

Inhumane: without compassion and humanity

Insane asylum: an old term for hospitals for the mentally ill, where conditions were often poor and many patients were held against their will

Leeches: bloodsucking worms formerly used in past eras of medicine

Lynching: murdering a person by mob action, often by hanging, without legal authority

Monarchy: supreme power held by a single person

Neonatal medicine: medical care for newborn infants

Philanthropist: a person who donates money or property to the needy

Polio: a viral disease that affects the brain stem and spinal cord that often causes paralysis

Quaker: a popular name for a member of the Society of Friends, a religious group originally founded in 17th-century England and known for its opposition to slavery and war

Recant: to withdraw a statement or opinion

Segregation: the separation of people based on race

Submissive: yielding to the authority of someone else

Suffrage: the right to vote

Temperance: moderation or abstinence from alcohol

Yellow fever: an often-fatal illness transmitted by mosquitos

RESOURCES

WEBSITES

Colonial Williamsburg Website – www.history.org
Mount Vernon Website – www.mountvernon.org
National Women's History Museum –
www.womenshistory.org
Smithsonian Learning Lab – learninglab.si.edu

BOOKS

A is for Awesome! 23 Iconic Women Who Changed the World by Eva Chen (New York: Feiwel & Friends, 2019)
Independent Dames: What You Never Knew About the Women and Girls of the American Revolution by Laurie Halse Anderson (New York: Simon & Schuster Books for Young Readers, 2008)
Little Leaders: Bold Women in Black History by Vashti Harrison (New York: Little Brown, 2017)

MUSEUMS

Colonial Williamsburg 18th Century Living History Museum in Williamsburg, Virginia
Ellis Island Immigration Museum in New York City
Mount Vernon Museum and Education Center in Virginia
National Civil Rights Museum in Memphis, Tennessee
Smithsonian National Museum of American History in Washington, DC

INDEX

ABOUT THE AUTHOR

Oklahoma-based upper elementary teacher Jenifer Bazzit creates social studies and writing curricula for Teachers Pay Teachers and her website, Thrive in Grade Five. With years of experience in making history accessible and engaging to students, she creates lessons that fuel students' fascination with history. Jenifer has a MEd in reading and visits historical sites often to expand her knowledge and find interesting tidbits to share with students.

AUTHOR ACKNOWLEDGMENTS

First, I want to thank the hundreds of students with whom I have worked. You are my inspiration for creating engaging lessons, and you've helped me become a better teacher every year.

Second, I want to recognize the many organizations and historical sites that have helped me bring history to life for students. I'd like to give special thanks to Colonial Williamsburg, Mount Vernon, the Gilder Lehrman Institute of American History, and the National Endowment for the Humanities for helping me fall in love with teaching history.

Third, I am so grateful to my elementary through high school teachers. Their high standards, kindness, and expertise made me want to be a teacher, too.

Most importantly, I'd like to thank my family for more than I could possibly list here: my husband and children, for being the biggest supporters of my creative efforts and the happiest part of every day; my parents, for instilling a love of reading and encouraging education; and my sisters (plus one sassy best friend who has become a sister) and brother for the adventures, coffee dates, and many laughs.

ABOUT THE ILLUSTRATOR

Steffi Walthall is an illustrator and character designer who has always been inspired by strong, fearless women, whether in history or in fiction. Steffi loves human-centric stories and creating images that celebrate and embrace diversity (and usually include a lady with a sword). When not working on a project, she can be found searching for inspiration in a book or out in nature with her Polaroid camera looking for another story to begin.

ILLUSTRATOR ACKNOWLEDGMENTS

Thank you to my incredible Pop and Gyoen. Pop, you've always believed in me and I am so grateful for everything you've done. Thank you to my wonderfully amazing twin sister Maeah and my incredibly brilliant little sis Faith. You both have been my constant motivation and inspiration. To my spectacular grandparents, Thelma and James, thank you for supporting my work even if you didn't always quite understand. To my phenomenal grandmother, Stephanie, thank you for always being my cheerleader and brightening up my day. And for my Granddaddy D, I hope I'm making you proud, I'll love you always.

CPSIA information can be obtained
at www.ICGtesting.com
Printed in the USA
BVHW050118131020
590845BV00006B/6